The
Emotional Rape
Syndrome

How To Survive and Avoid It

The Emotional Rape Syndrome

How To Survive and Avoid It

Michael Fox, Ph.D.

The Emotional Rape Syndrome,
How To Survive and Avoid It.

Library of Congress Cataloging in Publication Data

Fox, Michael.
       The Emotional Rape Syndrome,
       How To Survive and Avoid It.

1. Psychotherapy/Recovery.

Library of Congress Catalog Card # 92-060014

ISBN 0-9632103-1-9

First Printing 1992
10 9 8 7 6 5 4 3

Published by:

Tucson Publishing,
9121 E. Tanque Verde Road Suite 105, PMB 322,
Tucson, Arizona 85749.

Printed and Bound in the United States of America.

for Shara

About the Author

Michael Fox obtained his doctorate degree in physical chemistry in 1972. He is a scientist whose work on a wide range of research topics has been published in a variety of highly respected journals over the past twenty years.

He has been involved in research and development throughout his career, working for some of the largest high-technology corporations in the world. His interest in emotional rape was spurred by the attempted suicide of a close friend.

He now lives in Tucson, Arizona, where he is actively engaged in research, consulting, writing, and expert witness work.

Acknowledgments

...to the many people who
shared their stories,
making this book possible.

Contents

Introduction

Shara, a 37-year-old saleswoman, stopped her car on a freeway overpass late one afternoon and stared down at the rush hour traffic below, deciding whether or not to jump.

Cheryl, the 44-year-old owner of a successful beauty salon, dressed in evening clothes, parked her new convertible in her garage and sat with the garage door closed behind her and the engine running.

Steve, a 47-year-old insurance executive, woke up one morning at his Los Angeles home and, instead of getting out of bed to go to work, lay curled in a fetal position, a .38 revolver by his side.

Shara, Cheryl and Steve did not know each other but they had shared a common experience that drove them to contemplate the ultimate decision: whether to live or to die.

Shara jumped into the fast-moving traffic and was killed. Cheryl and Steve chose life, knowing they would have to face up to the experiences that had driven them to the brink of suicide and that their lives would never be the same again.

Both realized they would have to recover from the shattering effects of possibly the most underrated traumatic experience of today; an experience which, remarkably, does not even have a name, but which can only be adequately characterized as "emotional rape."

Unlike sexual rape, emotional rape is an experience which the victim is not aware of until, possibly many years after the damaging process began, the ambitions of the perpetrator—the rapist—are achieved or the ongoing hidden agenda is threatened with discovery. In either event the victim is left, after an inevitable and painful period of revelation, to cope with the traumatic consequences.

This book is about identifying and preventing emotional rape. Its purpose is to reassure victims that they didn't do anything morally wrong, that they are not to blame for what happened to them, and that recovery is possible.

Only after the characteristics of emotional rape are recognized and understood will it be possible for victims to recover, and to prevent the patterns of behavior involved.

Emotional rape is so much a part of our culture that we are not only blind to it, we also sanction and promote it.

Victims often cannot adequately express what has happened to them and so cannot come to terms with their situation. They know they are confused and depressed, hurt and enraged, but they don't know why, or what to do to recover.

The examples in this book are taken from real life cases. Those involved have been given different names, other details which might identify individuals have been disguised, and in some instances composite identities have been created to avoid any resemblance to specific persons or situations. But the emotional content of the stories is true: real people felt the pain, real people had to find ways to overcome the trauma and learn how to live again.

Cheryl's experience is recounted fully in Chapter Two and the circumstances that led to Shara's tragic death are examined in Chapter Three.

Chapter One deals with Steve's story—one which clearly illustrates the principal characteristics of emotional rape. The fact that the victim was male and the rapist female also demonstrates how this behavior is not confined to the typical gender boundaries of physical rape.

What is Emotional Rape? – a Classic Case

A Marriage of Convenience

Steve was 41 when he met Ellen. She was a twice-divorced 34-year-old mother of an 11-year-old boy. Steve had been married once before. Ellen had filed bankruptcy in her last marriage but told Steve she was beginning what was sure to be a lucrative career in sales.

He fell in love with her and after a few months they started living together.

Ellen's sales career was not as easily launched as she had suggested it would be, but Steve willingly supported her and her son financially. After all, he told himself, he had a good job and a reasonable income, and as her close emotional companion saw no reason to withhold his support in any area of their lives.

He was committed to her, convinced they were building a loving relationship that would last for many years, possibly for their entire lives. Two years later he and Ellen were married.

Before their marriage Ellen had dabbled in amateur drama productions and soon began to express an even greater interest in the theater.

She devoted more and more of her time to drama classes, explaining to Steve that acting was simply something she loved to do—nothing more than a hobby.

Although he told Ellen of his concern about the time and money she put into her acting, Steve remained supportive, always believing that such support was one expression of their loving relationship.

His financial help enabled Ellen to pay for her classes and in the four years following their marriage she spent $40,000 on professional drama training. Eventually she became sufficiently accomplished as an actress to support herself, but it proved to be an investment in time, money and emotional commitment which paid off only for Ellen.

Thinking he had a near-perfect marriage, Steve never suspected that his wife's real ambitions—for herself and their relationship—were very different from his own; that she had a hidden agenda, established when they first met, which was to pursue an acting career and to do whatever was necessary to achieve that goal.

The disintegration of their relationship, when the period of revelation began, was quick and complete.

A few weeks after the couple celebrated their fourth wedding anniversary, Steve had to be admitted to the hospital for minor surgery and unexpected complications resulted in an unplanned overnight stay. Even so, full recovery would require only about a week and Steve looked forward to returning home the next day.

However, when he got home to his wife and stepson he encountered a chilling, rather than caring, reception.

That same afternoon, instead of helping with Steve's recuperation, Ellen went to the theater and then to a girl-friend's house until the early evening. On her return she told him she would be going to a theater picnic the next day, leaving him alone again. Hardly able to walk, even using crutches, Steve was obviously not expected to join the party. When he questioned Ellen's priorities she announced that she was bored with their marriage.

The conversations which followed elicited a series of revelations about her true motivation and ambition, revelations of deceit throughout their relationship which left Steve in a state of shocked disbelief.

Finally it became obvious to him that she wanted their marriage to last one more year, so her son could graduate from a prestigious high school in their district.

For Steve, with their relationship exposed as anything but the honest and loving partnership he had imagined it to be, the prospect of a continuing "marriage of convenience" was intolerable.

He made this clear and within two weeks of his surgery he and Ellen agreed to separate. The marriage was over and almost immediately all Steve's love turned to rage.

He was confused, depressed and, while he had no tangible evidence at the time that he had been "used," the feeling was so real it made him vomit. He lost twenty pounds in thirty days and was on the verge of suicide.

The Hidden Agenda

It cannot be argued that every relationship which comes to an end is a case of emotional rape. So what distinguishes this situation from the many other circumstances which bring relationships to a painful end?

Isn't it possible that Steve and Ellen just grew apart, that theirs was a love story that simply didn't work out?

Perhaps Steve was an extremely difficult person to be involved with and, in truth, lucky the marriage lasted as long as it did. Where does the true story of the relationship lie? And in what way can Steve's experience legitimately be described as a violation analogous to rape?

The most significant distinguishing feature of emotional rape—one discovered in material form by Steve—is the presence of a hidden, or dishonest, agenda.

Months later, while he was searching through records

to prepare for divorce proceedings, Steve found a five-year-old diary belonging to Ellen. This journal spelled out her plans to pursue an acting career, plans she had never shared with him although he had repeatedly asked about the long-term purpose of her expensive and time-consuming interest in the theater.

The discovery of that diary—a statement of intent—clarified beyond doubt Ellen's selfish motives for her involvement with Steve. She had deliberately used his love and support as a vehicle to move towards her own secret goal of becoming an actress.

This is the classic emotional rape scenario: the use of a higher emotion (in this case, love) to fulfill a hidden agenda (her acting career).

Even after their separation, when, although she didn't know it, Steve had read her diary, Ellen still insisted that she never planned a full time acting career, saying it was simply something that had happened "one step at a time."

Her continued denial of the existence of any hidden agenda showed the depth of her deception and led Steve to the painful realization that she had never loved him.

There can be no hidden agendas in real love.

A sincere relationship requires agreements between partners. The exact nature of these agreements—whether they are written, spoken, or implied understandings—is not important. What is important is that there *is* understanding and trust between the people involved.

Between a man and a woman the most common agreements are that their relationship will be lasting, honest and monogamous. When one partner's intentions are at odds with these understandings, and are kept secret from the other partner, the relationship becomes basically flawed.

In cases of emotional rape this dishonesty is often present from the very beginning, although it is unusual to find hard evidence, as Steve did, of the hidden agenda.

(Emotional rapists tend to avoid any definite spoken or written statements of intent, preferring vaguely-defined implied agreements.)

However, a sufficient number of identifiable characteristics are usually present that, while it is often too late for catastrophe to be anticipated and averted, the reasons for the breakdown of the relationship can be understood after the event.

These features, even if identified in retrospect, can help victims understand what has happened to them, giving them a chance of real recovery.

Significant Features

There are two other significant features of emotional rape, the first being sudden reversal.

The victim thinks the relationship is fine until this illusion is unexpectedly shattered, typically when the ambitions of the rapist have been achieved, or when he or she realizes the success of the hidden agenda is threatened.

This was evident in the story of Steve and Ellen. She had completed her hidden agenda, and her true priorities were exposed when he returned home after surgery and needed her to care for him.

The second characteristic is that victims feel extremely "used" and fear they will never be able to love or trust again.

For Steve this feeling was so overwhelming that it made him vomit. It is this devastating effect that emotional rape has upon the individual that absolutely justifies the use of the word "rape" to describe the experience.

But is it Rape?

Why not simply identify relationships such as Steve's and Ellen's as "exploitive relationships"? The answer is readily apparent: for the same reason we don't call torture a form of physical persuasion.

"Rape" is the only word which adequately conveys the trauma experienced by the victim; one of the few words in our language, as one writer astutely observed, "with the power to summon a shared image of a horrible crime.".

To use a word with less impact would grossly misrepresent the degree of trauma suffered by the victim, thus underestimating the complexity of the emotions he or she must come to terms with before recovery can begin.

Research suggests that a person can certainly experience many of the accepted symptoms of post-traumatic rape syndrome without being sexually raped.

For example, just twenty-four hours after Ellen moved out, Steve removed from the house every item which belonged to her. Within a week he had every room cleaned, painted and re-carpeted.

He couldn't explain why he felt compelled to get rid of Ellen's belongings and "sterilize" his home, which he had owned prior to his marriage to Ellen. However, this impulse corresponds to a reaction commonly felt by victims of sexual rape: the sterilization of his house was a subconscious attempt to "get clean."

The breakup caused Steve to suffer severe trauma. Not only had he lost someone he loved, causing a sense of loss and yearning for that loved one, but he also felt anger and rage at having been used by that person.

Emotional rape leaves victims wrestling with these powerful and conflicting emotions which when they collide—rather as two cars might crash head-on—leave a tangled mass of human wreckage that seriously threatens the ability to love and trust anyone in the future.

Toward a Definition

It is instructive to compare the characteristics and effects of sexual rape with those involved in emotional rape. Two working definitions might be:

- Sexual rape is the sexual use of someone's body without that person's consent.
- Emotional rape is the use of someone's higher emotions without that person's consent.

The higher emotions taken advantage of include love, trust, caring, generosity, honor, loyalty, innocence, patriotism, achievement and faith.

The payoff—the satisfaction for the emotional rapist—can take many forms, including financial gain, education, security, sex, excitement, job advancement, a sense of power or control, and even time.

In Steve's case the higher emotion used was love.

Ellen's payoff was gaining her education and training as an actress and having a surrogate father for her son during his most difficult teenage years.

This book focuses principally on the most common form of emotional rape, which occurs between a man and a woman and uses love. However, this destructive behavior is by no means confined to that pattern.

The rapist can be male or female, a spouse or a lover, but also in some instances a parent, child, friend, employer—even a corporation, religion or government.

Many Vietnam war veterans are still struggling to cope with the traumatic experiences they went through, having been exploited by a government that used their higher emotions of patriotism, honor, duty and courage. (This example is discussed more fully in later chapters.)

Victims, too, can be as varied as the rapists: male or female, young or old, married or single.

Violation of the Soul

The key words in these basic definitions are "use" and "without consent."

What gets "used" in emotional rape—and how this is done without consent—has no real analogy in sexual rape where the abuse can be more easily described: the physical body is violated.

The violation in emotional rape is more subtle because the parts of an individual that are abused—the higher emotions of love or trust, for example—are not tangible.

In sexual rape the words "without consent" refer to the victim having withheld something, having not freely agreed to sex. In contrast it is the perpetrator, the rapist, who withholds something in emotional rape, employing deceit to conceal his or her true motives.

If sexual rape is the violation of the human body, emotional rape is the violation of the human soul.

The Limits of Logic

Anyone who has been a victim of emotional rape will readily understand how it is possible to be totally unaware of another person's hidden agenda, even in an apparently close relationship.

However, those who have not experienced such a situation often find it incomprehensible that someone could be so completely deceived. They argue logically that involvement in a close relationship is, by definition, incompatible with the idea that one partner could conceal his or her true motives from the other, particularly over a significant period of time.

It can be extremely difficult for such rational individuals to accept the idea of emotional rape.

Rather, they might question whether the victim did not in some way consent to their own exploitation, either directly or indirectly. (A similar question is often asked of victims of alleged date rape.)

However, throughout history the application of logic and reason alone has failed to provide any comprehensive explanation for the possibilities of human relationships.

It is worth recalling one recent case, the story of a New Hampshire high school teacher, Pamela Smart, who seduced a teenage boy and persuaded him to murder her husband.

This young woman was certainly capable of concealing her true motives, and not only from her husband but from his family as well. Media coverage after his death focused in part upon the sympathy and support Pamela Smart received from her husband's family and friends before the truth was known about her role in his murder.

It was a tragic case of accomplished manipulation, dishonesty and ultimately death; one which illustrates how hidden agendas *can* be concealed, even from those apparently closest to the deceiver.

Analogies and Priorities

There are two generalized categories of sexual rape: stranger rape and acquaintance rape, which includes date rape.

Stranger rape is illegal and there is a strong social stigma which attaches to those who are convicted by a court of this offense.

Date rape is also illegal, although it is difficult to prove and how it is perceived in the public mind is unclear. Certainly, being accused of date rape does not automatically attract the same degree of popular condemnation as being charged with stranger rape. The suggestion will often be made that the victim of date rape might in some way have been responsible for, or a willing participant in, what took place.

In contrast, almost all cases of emotional rape are perfectly legal.

The emotional rapist may even be widely admired. It's a telling commentary on society's moral priorities that a person who exploits someone's affections for personal gain—in pursuit of money or an education, for example—might well be considered a shrewd entrepreneur rather than a villain.

Time Factors

Sexual rape generally occurs over a short, well-defined period of time whereas emotional rape is typically, though not exclusively, perpetrated gradually, over a long period.

Many of the case studies in this book occurred over five years or longer and the extended time span contributes to the difficulties we have identifying instances of emotional rape. It also causes victims to feel uncertain about what exactly happened to them, a confusion which is likely to delay their recovery.

It should be noted, however, that emotional rape can take place over a short period of time. For example, a woman may feel its traumatic effects after a sexual encounter, even though she freely consented to sex.

She may have believed she was involved in a truly loving relationship with the man when, in fact, her affections were only being exploited to fulfill his hidden agenda of physical gratification. In agreeing to sex, she thought she was taking the next step in their relationship, but to her partner it was the final step.

The Self-Blame Fallacy

Sexual rape invariably leaves victims concerned about being alone, about the motivation of strangers, and wary of everyone except their most trusted friends and their families.

Emotional rape may leave victims unable to trust anyone, with the exception of their closest family and long-term friends—and even they may be suspect.

Victims of emotional rape can't psychologically protect themselves from feelings of isolation by attributing what happened to the abhorrent and exceptional behavior of one individual, as a victim of stranger rape might be able to do.

Instead, more like the victims of date rape, they may begin to question themselves, doubting their own judgment and values.

In some instances they will be encouraged to embark on this process of self-blame.

Friends, family members, and even some professional counselors often make well-meaning, but potentially extremely damaging, observations; something along the lines of "What is it about you which is attracted to a person like that?" or "How did you fail to see what he/she was up to?"

As a result, victims of emotional rape invariably come to see themselves as responsible for what happened.

They do not recognize that what happened to them was rape, rather they rationalize that it was simply an instance of personal failing. This is a destructive fallacy.

Realization and Diagnosis

The characteristics common to cases of emotional rape have never been examined as a whole area of human experience. Yet it is only through an awareness of these identifying characteristics—the realization that "Yes, this is what really happened to me"—that victims can begin to recover from its traumatic effects.

And *is* this really what happened? Only the individual

concerned can answer that question, by applying the criteria for what constitutes emotional rape to his or her own experience. However, two things are certain:

A correct diagnosis is essential for recovery from any illness, physical or emotional.

And anyone who has ever suffered a prolonged undiagnosed condition knows the sense of relief which follows when that condition is finally given a name.

The Aftermath

The Final Blow

Seated in her new convertible, the engine running and the garage door closed behind her, Cheryl was on the point of taking her own life.

She was desperately aware that something terrible had happened to her—an experience which shattered her life and now threatened to end it—but she had no idea how to describe what had occurred, or how she might be able to recover if, indeed, recovery was possible. She was facing up to the aftermath of emotional rape.

Robert had been particularly brutal when he ended their six-year relationship.

Having used Cheryl's love to gain a convenient escort, a sexual partner, a temporary mother for his children, a housekeeper, and expensive vacations, his hidden agenda had been fulfilled. It was time to move on. He had found a wealthier Ms. Right, but to avoid being seen by friends and family as responsible for the breakup he tried to maneuver Cheryl into the position of ending the relationship.

He began treating her with a complete lack of respect, ignoring her when she spoke to him, always disagreeing with her choice of places to go, and frequently arriving late, or not at all.

Because she loved him and had faith in their future together Cheryl tolerated this sudden day-to-day thoughtlessness, believing it was simply a temporary interruption of their normal relationship, so Robert was forced to become increasingly open about his own intentions.

He delivered the final blow just before a graduation party for one of his children, when Cheryl called him to discuss their plans for the event.

She asked what time he wanted her to pick him up so they could travel together. He said she wouldn't have to bother. When she asked whether he had already arranged a ride he replied: "No, I have a date."

It was this brief conversation that signaled the start of the nightmare that took Cheryl to the brink of suicide.

Colliding Emotions

It is no exaggeration to describe emotional rape as the most underrated trauma of our age; the effects are powerful and potentially destructive.

Victims like Cheryl are forced to cope with a tangle of conflicting emotions, experiencing all the traumatic aftereffects of both rape and loss.

This confused pattern of emotional responses is very similar to that experienced by victims of sexual rape.

It's a pattern commonly identified as post-traumatic rape syndrome, although victims of emotional rape will be unaware that this is what is happening to them.

These colliding emotions become so entangled that it is extremely difficult—and would be a serious misrepresentation—to attempt to categorize them individually. They are inseparable.

However, it is possible to identify certain generalized feelings which characterize the emotional aftermath.

Principally, these are:

- **Denial**
- **Isolation**
- **Feeling 'Had' or 'Used'**
- **Loneliness**
- **Rage and Obsession**
- **Inability to Love or Trust**
- **Fear and Anxiety**
- **Loss of Self-Esteem**
- **Confusion**
- **Erratic Behavior**
- **Hidden and Delayed Reactions**

Each of these is considered in detail in this chapter, as are the typical physical and material aftereffects, so victims will understand that what they are going through is normal, that they are not alone, and that they are not insane. Later chapters examine how to recover from many of these symptoms.

Denial

Denial is a main aftereffect of emotional rape and manifests itself in many forms. One form is self-blame.

We have a natural tendency to accept responsibility for what happens to us because we want to believe we are always in full control of our lives. When bad things happen, rather than admit they might have occurred because of some outside, non-controllable, set of circumstances, we prefer to believe our own actions were the cause. We blame ourselves.

For example, Cheryl was unaware that she had been emotionally raped; her experience had not been identified as one perpetrated by Robert against her, without her knowledge or consent. So it seemed to her that the anguish she was feeling must have been caused by her own actions and weaknesses.

Indeed, she prefaced her story by listing her own shortcomings. But she was the victim—she had been emotionally raped.

Her intentions and motives had always been honest. His hidden agenda, his dishonest intent, had been indisputably present from the outset, and having achieved the goals of that agenda he precipitated the breakup of their relationship. This is the hallmark of an emotional rape situation.

Nevertheless, for a long time Cheryl continued to accept much of the blame for what had happened, an acceptance which prevented her from beginning the process of recovery.

Emotional rape victims have a two-fold responsibility to themselves: to resist the natural tendency toward self-blame, and not to unquestioningly accept the critical judgments of others.

There is a widespread attitude in our society that the victim in such cases must be the one who is to blame, a feeling which encourages individuals to blame themselves for everything which happens to them.

But there is a huge volume of empirical evidence, in the form of case studies, which shows that this "victim-is-guilty" presumption is not infallible.

Not every unhappy situation, tragic occurrence, or traumatic experience is the result of personal weakness or choice. Outside influences do act upon the individual.

The closing advice of the previous chapter is worthy of frequent repetition:

When asking, "Was my experience emotional rape?" examine only whether the basic characteristics of emotional rape were present or absent within the relationship. If those characteristics were present, acceptance of blame serves no useful purpose and, moreover, is extremely damaging.

Certainly, there is a time and place for a victim to

ponder on how what happened could possibly have been prevented, but there is also an important difference between healthy self-examination and unhealthy, counterproductive self-blame.

Isolation

A woman raped by a stranger can often hold on to a sense—even if it is very fragile— that the people she knows provide a zone of protection and support. Her experience as a victim may be validated by the sympathetic reactions of the people close to her. However, for a woman [sexually] raped by a man she knows (date rape), this zone is often missing. Like a stranger rape victim, her confidence in the world has been upended; unlike a stranger rape victim, few people will offer a date rape victim sympathy due to the social myths about date rape, the tendency to blame the victim, and her own likelihood to keep silent about the rape.

—Robin Warshaw, *I Never Called It Rape.*

This extract points out a distinctive difference between the aftermath of date rape and stranger rape. It also warns of a significant similarity between emotional rape and sexual date rape: in neither case can victims rely on any useful support system to help cope with their trauma.

Frequently there is no "zone of protection and support" for victims of emotional rape—making the essential transition from victim to survivor especially difficult.

For similar reasons, emotional rape can be even more difficult to come to terms with than bereavement.

Next to the death of a loved one, the ending of a precious relationship is the most traumatic event we can experience—but at least in the case of bereavement there is some small consolation in knowing that those left behind were loved by the deceased, and the mourners are treated sympathetically by friends and family.

In contrast, the individual who loses someone through emotional rape is, by definition, denied any consoling feeling of having been loved. On the contrary, the predominant feeling is of having been "used" by the departed, by the rapist, and often there is little real understanding among friends and family.

The aftermath of emotional rape leaves victims struggling with all the disabling effects of both loss and rape, but without any useful comfort zone in which escape or relief might be possible.

Feeling 'Had' or 'Used'

Many victims spontaneously use the word "rape" to describe what has happened to them. One woman actually used the phrase "emotional rape," even though she had never heard that term before. The experience just felt like that to her.

Just like those who have been sexually raped, emotional rape victims commonly feel "had" or "used" and frequently feel a need to try to "get clean," although this cleansing process is not necessarily focused on the body.

As we saw in Chapter One, Steve "sterilized" his house, repainting inside and out, laying new carpets, hanging new pictures on the walls and buying new furniture. Others have burned photographs, thrown away clothes, and smashed personal belongings.

Outsiders can contribute to the feeling of being "used." There are psychiatrists and therapists, for example, who will listen intently to their patients up to the allotted time, then, with a glance at the clock, abruptly conclude the session: "That will be $100. See you next week."

Such an approach may seem all the more callous because of the victim's sensitive condition. (It should be remembered, however, that any professionals who are sought out for assistance, whether they are therapists or attorneys, have to remain emotionally detached if they are to provide the most effective service to their clients.)

Loneliness

One victim said she had an out-of-body experience that intensified her already acute sense of isolation to an almost unbearable degree:

"I was lying on the bed face down and had the sensation of falling into a black hole in space. The darkness and sense of aloneness were indescribable. I was the only one in the entire universe and it was the most terrifying experience of my life. I would rather be burning in hell, as long as there was someone with me."

Her use of the phrase "black hole" is significant, evoking the immensity of the void she felt after her partner's deceit was revealed.

In modern Western society we still typically have one primary, close relationship, usually with our spouse or lover. If that person is exposed as a rapist the void left behind can, indeed, be of cosmic proportions and the inclination to withdraw emotionally is a natural reaction.

Very few, if any, victims of emotional rape fully understand what has happened to them and they may be reluctant to discuss their feelings with others for fear they will simply encourage criticism of their "weakness."

An individual does not have to be physically alone to feel such loneliness.

After her breakup with Robert, Cheryl bought that glamorous new convertible and went out on dates almost every night. Being attractive and outgoing, well-dressed and a good dancer, she had little difficulty finding interested partners; but she still felt alone and unloved.

Her soul was isolated. She was caught in a painful Catch-22 situation: lonely, yet her efforts to relieve this loneliness caused further anxiety because she could not get close to others. She was unaware that she was experiencing post-traumatic rape syndrome.

Rage and Obsession

Many victims freely admit to being obsessively preoccupied with feelings of anger towards the person who perpetrated the rape. It is a readily understandable and justifiable obsession, a feeling just as intense as the anger of someone who has been sexually raped or assaulted.

However, it can exacerbate the situation, particularly when they face the "mirror of blame" unknowingly erected by friends and family, and the message reflected is that they have no one to blame but themselves. Forced to cope with this verdict on their situation they may direct their anger back on to themselves, starting on yet another downward curve in the spiral of self-doubt.

Consuming anger can also spill over into other areas of life, with serious consequences. One victim found he was getting into increasingly tense confrontations with a vice president at his work The slightest stress would trigger his angry response and he eventually had to take a leave of absence on medical grounds.

Personal relationships can suffer, at the very time when the positive support and understanding of friends and family are most needed. Even those closest to the victim may not sufficiently appreciate what he or she is going through to tolerate too many apparently irrational outbursts of temper.

The situation becomes even more fraught if the victim feels some bitterness towards those close to him, or her, because of their failure to understand what has happened.

However, anger can be a powerful motivating force, a source of strength, when it is controlled and put to constructive use—a strategy discussed later in detail.

Inability to Love or Trust

You used to think you had good judgment, but maybe you didn't if you chose that man to spend time with; you trusted him, and look what happened. If you had had better judgment, you wouldn't have chosen him as someone desirable and safe to spend time with. Trust in personal judgment and in others is gone. This is especially likely if the victim told her family or friends about the rape and they blamed her for it or did not believe her.

—Andrea Parrot, *Coping with Date Rape & Acquaintance Rape.*

Self-doubt affects the victim's ability to trust others, and here again the aftereffects of date rape closely parallel those of emotional rape.

(Note that for "man" here, we can substitute "woman," for "her" we can substitute "him." Emotional rape, as stated earlier, is not confined to the typical gender roles of physical rape.)

The loss of the ability to love or trust is probably the most damaging effect of emotional rape.

When the ability to give love is damaged, even temporarily, the loss is felt immediately.

Love is one of those paradoxical wonders that a person gets by giving it away, felt most purely when it is generated for someone else.

The individual who is unable to trust or love has been wounded by a double-edged sword: he or she is incapable of giving trust or love, and is therefore incapable of experiencing these feelings. Paradoxically, this incapacity occurs when that individual most needs to reach out to others and be comforted by their support.

Fear and Anxiety

Emotional rape victims will be preoccupied with many fears and concerns: fears of being alone, about the strength of their feelings of anger and rage, anxieties about starting a new relationship or their capacity for ever loving again.

There may be serious concerns about tangible losses; perhaps money which has been lost, or career opportunities which have been passed by. They may worry what other people think, about how friends and family might react if they are told what is really going on.

All these fears must be expected and accepted.

If prospects for the future seem particularly bleak, victims may also feel that they have nothing to live for, that life is meaningless, and perhaps even that they have been abandoned by God.

This can have tragic consequences because the one fear that may actually be diminished amid the trauma is the fear of death, or of taking one's own life. That most victims at some point contemplate suicide is grim proof of this readiness to accept mortality.

One businesswoman who frequently had to fly to meetings in distant cities confessed that in the aftermath of her emotional rape experience she no longer felt the tension she used to during takeoff and landing maneuvers.

"What the hell," she said. "I don't have anything to live for anyway, so why bother getting upset about the plane crashing?"

Loss of Self-Esteem

The emotional rape victim suffers a serious loss of self-esteem and, feeling isolated from others—even fearful of becoming the subject of their criticism—may descend into a dangerous downward spiral which leads in some cases to self-loathing, feelings of hopelessness, and suicide.

Self-criticism, in moderation as self-awareness, is a valuable character trait—taken to extremes it can be fatal.

Victims of emotional rape typically feel unworthy, unloved, unlovable, fat, skinny, ugly, too tall, too short, too weak, too strong, too bald, too old, too young, too poor, too emotional, or too unemotional. They are also particularly vulnerable to further victimization by another emotional rapist because of their desperate need to have self-esteem restored, to be validated by anyone.

Confusion

Another step towards recovery is to recognize that confused behavior is normal under the circumstances.

Victims cite numerous everyday examples: missing freeway exits, forgetting skillets left on a hot stove, losing personal items (like eyeglasses and purses), locking the keys in the car, forgetting appointments, not remembering why you went into a particular room in your house, forgetting what you did for short periods of time... The list is a long one.

Those with a particularly demanding job will find themselves less able to concentrate and may become aware of a dramatic drop in their productivity.

Less obvious, however, is the internal confusion which prompts consideration of the nature of love and the purpose of life.

This commonly arises when a particularly clever rapist has so successfully manipulated and distorted the basic truth that the victim is unable to distinguish fact from fiction.

Erratic Behavior

Irrational and extreme behavior is also to be expected.

In her state of emotional turmoil, Cheryl felt life was no longer worth living. Yet she spent thousands of dollars on a new car and pitched herself headlong into a dating "frenzy" in a fruitless search for a replacement partner.

Some victims go into complete withdrawal, isolating themselves physically as well as emotionally. Some recall having existed in a prolonged state of emotional "numbness."

Others go on spending sprees, devotees of the theory that going out and buying something new can be therapeutic—which is often true if the purchase is reasonable and affordable. Buying a "treat" can help to rebuild self-esteem and provide a feeling of control.

However if the shopping habit is too extravagantly indulged it becomes a serious problem in itself. Many victims admit having bought expensive new cars, linking their sense of self-worth to the value of their automobiles. Some may buy whole new wardrobes, furniture, or exclusive cosmetics.

Exercise equipment and electronic goods like video players and televisions are typical purchases, items which hold the promise of a new direction in life, a renewal or fresh start for the victim, but which, when the first purchases fail to fill the emotional void, can lead to compulsive spending and economic ruin.

Any latent addictions, which give immediate gratification and create a temporary sense of safety and security, may also become full-blown obsessions.

For example, one man who had given up cigarettes twenty years before started smoking up to two packs a day. The compulsion to smoke overtook him almost instantly. Others have reported addictive behavior involving sex, alcohol and drugs.

Hidden and Delayed Reactions

People who have been emotionally raped may be subject to hidden reactions.

If love was the higher emotion exploited, an uplifting romantic movie on television can arouse intense feelings of loss or sadness, and because the individual is unaware of the reasons for these negative responses this can lead to a more general feeling of depression.

Here again, the experiences of victims of emotional rape are analogous to those of date rape victims.

The following example of date rape illustrates the importance of recognizing the reality of hidden reactions:

Brenda, an intelligent and attractive woman in her late-thirties, was seriously troubled by the inexplicable discomfort she felt just being in the presence of a man. She would accept dates, but pulled away at the slightest hint of physical contact. Even at dinner she would sit as far away from her companion as possible.

Brenda had been a victim of date rape, but for a year afterwards did not recognize that experience as rape. She felt that she was to blame, that she had been careless in her behavior and that it had been largely her own fault.

The indisputable fact, however, was that she had not freely consented to sex and, although she continued to like the company of men, she subconsciously felt a need to keep her distance from them. It was only when she began to accept that she had been raped that she was able to begin relating normally again to her male friends.

Delayed reactions are also common.

Significantly, many Vietnam war veterans exhibited the characteristic signs of post-traumatic rape syndrome during the Iran-Contra hearings in the late 1980s. (Emotional rape, as noted in Chapter One, is not confined to intimate relationships between two individuals. This is the most common context, but our higher emotions can be exploited by group entities, such as a corporation or a government.)

The trigger which exposed these latent, unresolved stresses during those hearings was primarily the television appearances of Marine Colonel Oliver North, whose unwavering belief in the principles of patriotism, honor, bravery and duty gained him widespread sympathy throughout the United States.

Colonel North exemplified all the higher emotions which had been used to emotionally rape the men and women sent to Vietnam. These highly visible aspects of his personality acted as keys to unlock the buried emotions of many Vietnam veterans.

In their tours of duty they had not had any opportunity to consider whether they were being "used." Even a quarter century later many veterans may not fully understand what happened to them. However, when people are emotionally raped and then repress their feelings there is always a likelihood that their trauma will surface—perhaps subtly, perhaps violently—some time afterwards.

Vietnam veterans instinctively identified with Colonel North, having in many respects a common experience of the emotions he displayed throughout his TV testimony.

Their understanding of his situation, on a very fundamental level, was evident in the phrases they employed to sum up their reaction to his predicament. These included: "He was used...He was just following orders, like we did...We were used...Yes, we were raped."

Their rapist was the government. The higher emotions exploited were patriotism, honor, duty, and courage. But only a small percentage of veterans got any useful therapy to help them deal with the traumatic aftermath of their experience—and it is not difficult to see why.

To arrange such treatment would involve at least a tacit admission by the government that those servicemen and women had been "used."

The Material Aftereffects

The emotional stress can trigger tangible changes:

Weight Loss or Gain
It is not uncommon for individuals to gain or lose a considerable amount of weight after the period of revelation. Following his breakup with Ellen, Steve lost twenty pounds in thirty days.

Symptomatic Illnesses
Among those recalled by survivors of emotional rape are insomnia, irritability, headaches, impotence and high blood pressure.

Addictive Behavior
Victims may become increasingly reliant upon alcohol, tobacco or other drugs.

There are also calculable material effects:

Financial Losses
These include the loss of money and property, and can have a lasting effect.

Cindy, whose husband was revealed as an emotional rapist, discovered that in their short marriage the $50,000 she had previously saved toward retirement had all been spent. There was little chance she would be able to rebuild her savings to that level.

In fact, even when she was legally separated from her husband he managed to buy a new $30,000 car—with her name on the loan. Quite unexpectedly she received a curt phone call from staff at the bank, demanding to know why the last two payments had not been made. The bank records showed her telephone number but not his.

Legal Expenses
As the prosecution of cases of sexual rape involves the victim in a very painful and expensive legal process of

depositions, testimony and trial, so, often, does the aftermath of emotional rape.

In some instances, just as the victim is beginning to recover, the rapist comes back for more. His or her presence during certain stages of the legal proceedings inevitably causes additional stress.

In the case of Steve and Ellen, after he had supported her dramatic aspirations to the figure of $40,000 spent on acting classes, she reappeared to contest their prenuptial agreement so she could get alimony.

She had discovered she could not earn sufficient money as an actress to support herself and returned seeking further, ongoing funding for her career. Steve, who was already experiencing severe emotional difficulties, was unable to cope with the ensuing legal wrangling and had to take extended personal leave from work.

Another victim recalled how, when she was deposed for her divorce and had to face her husband in person, the proceedings left her physically and emotionally exhausted. She collapsed for the remainder of the day because simply walking from one room to another caused her to have dizzy spells.

Not all the tangible losses of emotional rape can be assigned a dollar value in, or out of, a courtroom:

Lost Time

There are some losses sustained in emotional rape that may be recovered or replaced. Time is not one of them.

Thelma, for example, spent five years in a relationship with Bill. He repeatedly told her how much he loved her, but said he was not ready to get married or have children. Then he suddenly announced he had changed his mind and that he was ready to enter into both those long-term commitments—with another woman.

It is impossible to calculate the loss of those five years, time wasted from the child-bearing years of a woman to whom starting a family was vitally important.

Victims also commonly lose irretrievable time when they pass up opportunities to develop their career, or their personal interests, because of their involvement with the rapist.

Lost Sympathies and Friends

The rapist's proven talent for persuading others to see in him, or her, only what he, or she, wants them to see may be a telling factor in the aftermath of emotional rape.

Typically, an emotional rapist has a confident, persuasive, often charismatic personality. And, being unaffected by the debilitating effects of trauma, he or she is perfectly situated to use those abilities to gain the sympathy of outsiders—at the expense of the victim.

These "outsiders" may be mutual friends of the rapist and victim, or, in cases involving legal confrontations, even the judge. Lawyers' offices and courtrooms are an ideal forum to practice such "skills" and establish credibility as anything other than a deceiver and manipulator.

How Long Does it Last?

The most telling observation cannot be stated too often: that a correct diagnosis, and an acceptance by the victim of what has happened, is essential before the healing process can begin.

Even then it is impossible to say how long recovery will take in each particular case. Everyone heals differently, and at a different rate, and the severity of the wounds caused by the experience varies considerably according to each situation.

One victim, who broke down in tears as she told her story, had been emotionally raped seven years before. Even after that time, her healing process had still not been completed, probably due to the lack of a correct diagnosis.

The passing of one full year is often a major turning

point, provided diagnosis is made soon after the rape is discovered.

Generally it takes longer to recover from emotional rape than from date rape, for the same reasons it takes longer to recover from date rape than from stranger rape: the degree of love and trust involved is much greater so the damage is inflicted at a deeper emotional level. The tangible losses—whether in money, property, time or any other aspect of life—are also likely to be greater.

Emotional rape can destroy any confidence in one's ability to judge what—or who—is safe. Victims restrict their emotions to protect themselves and only tentatively test human nature in the attempt to restore their sense of emotional safety.

Nevertheless, that sense can be regained, and life can be even more joyous than before. It takes both time and courage, but the ability to function again as a whole human being is a payoff which makes any investment of time and effort worthwhile.

Profiles of Rapists and Victims

3

It Could Happen to Anyone

Shara, who died after jumping from a freeway overpass into rush hour traffic, was exploited by a rapist who could accurately be described as armed and dangerous; an accomplished deceiver who had raped before.

Without exception, victims describe two predominant characteristics of their rapists:

They are charismatic, ostensibly attractive personalities, likely to be widely admired, but with a naturally manipulative nature.

They can completely conceal their true selves.

These two observations draw attention to one of the central features of such behavior:

Emotional rape can happen to anyone. The widely varying backgrounds and personalities of those who have already become victims demonstrate the danger in thinking otherwise; in believing "It could never happen to me."

It is sometimes difficult to believe that no moral responsibility rests with the victim—because he or she was weak, naive, or otherwise "to blame"—but that it lies with the rapist, whose ability to conceal his or her true self is such that almost anyone could be deceived.

The next chapter (which addresses the question, What Makes Emotional Rape Possible?) looks at the reasons why such a wide range of people are vulnerable to this traumatic experience.

The focus here is mainly on the rapist, examining what it is that makes an individual capable of this form of psychological aggression.

A History of Deception

Brent gained Shara's love and trust by employing his knowledge as a doctor of psychology, and his undoubted personal charisma, with lethal efficiency.

When he had successfully seduced her, he manipulated her and exercised his power over her to vent his secret hatred of women. Like most emotional, and sexual, rapists he was motivated more by the need for total control in his relationships than by a desire to gain tangible assets, or basic sexual gratification.

He displayed most of the classic characteristics of an emotional rapist. Furthermore, his background as a rapist in at least one relationship before he became involved with Shara was well documented.

Victim #1: Barbara

For almost six years before meeting Shara, Brent was involved with Barbara, a criminal psychologist by profession and a particularly "street-smart" individual by nature.

One of the most disturbing realizations for Barbara was that, even with all her training, she had been unaware that she was being deceived, in all probability over a long period of time. After all, it was vital in her job to be able to tell whether someone was speaking the truth or lying. Yet, after hearing Brent assure her of his fidelity and love, she knew she would never have suspected he was lying—if she had not got incontrovertible proof.

Damning Evidence

Their relationship had its fair share of short-term separations, always initiated by Brent, followed by reconciliation; again, at his suggestion.

Periodically, he would announce that their relationship was over, or simply disappear without explanation. Barbara would be left alone and devastated by these sudden twists and turns in her emotional life.

Then he would reappear and, because she was deeply in love with him, Barbara would take him back, justifying her actions to herself by believing such painful upsets would not continue forever. (Whether Barbara was simply naïve, or whether her behavior was driven by deep human needs, is a question dealt with later in the book.)

Brent was exploiting his partner's love for him to gratify his need for control over women. The periodic breakups were essential for him to experience complete gratification.

Despite her innate belief in the strength of their feelings for each other, as the years passed, Barbara became increasingly suspicious that there was something abnormal in their relationship. Eventually, she asked Brent if he was involved with another woman, a suggestion he vigorously denied, reassuring her that he was in love with her.

What he did not know was that Barbara had hired a private detective to investigate his mysterious absences, and she knew he was seeing another woman.

The Rapist as Manipulator

Barbara chose not to immediately confront Brent with the evidence of his betrayal because she knew she needed a few days to sort out her confused feelings. And, although later it was painful for her to admit, she also fondly hoped she might find a way to keep their relationship alive because she was still very much in love.

However, her questions must have been a signal to Brent that his hidden agenda and dishonesty were about to be exposed. Ever the manipulator, within two days he precipitated the breakup of their relationship—and managed to cast her as the one responsible.

When they first met, six years earlier, Barbara was forty-five, two years older than Brent, and had three children. She told him she had no real desire to have more children and from that moment on Brent had given no indication that he ever wanted to become a father. That is, until his paternal instincts were suddenly, and conveniently, aroused.

Quite unexpectedly, he telephoned Barbara and informed her he now wanted to start a family of his own. He said her reluctance to become a mother for a fourth time had become a major problem and, because of her attitude, he had decided their relationship must end. He made her feel she was to blame.

He would not admit to Barbara that he was involved with another woman and wanted to move on. Instead, suspecting he was about to be discovered, he manufactured a confrontational situation which left Barbara in emotional shambles. This is a typical ploy.

Having achieved the goals of his or her hidden agenda, the rapist hides behind a carefully crafted "cover story." He or she appears to outsiders to be the calm, cool one—a role that contrasts favorably with that of the victim, who has been maneuvered into a state of emotional instability.

Victim #2: Shara

In time, Barbara learned more and more about Brent—and about his next victim, Shara.

The detective Barbara had hired, a woman, had become more of a friend than an employee, and regularly checked on Brent's telephone messages after breaking the code of his answering machine.

From the messages left by Shara, it became clear that he was using the same methods, the same charm and lies, he had used on Barbara. And when, finally, he chose to end this relationship, he created an almost identical confrontation: Shara could not have children, he had suddenly decided he wanted a family of his own, so she was responsible for the breakup.

In each new telephone message that she left for Brent, Shara sounded increasingly distressed.

Clearly, she was completely distraught. Barbara was about to contact her, to try to help her survive the situation, when Shara drove her car the short distance from her apartment to the freeway overpass and jumped into speeding traffic.

Further investigations by the private detective revealed that at the outset of their relationship, one of Shara's closest friends warned Brent she had a childhood history of emotional abuse, was extremely vulnerable, and could be unstable under extreme stress.

She had obviously never been a good candidate for marriage or motherhood. However, Brent's needs for power, control and ego gratification were more important to him than Shara's well-being.

He methodically pursued his hidden agenda in the relationship with the same calculating ruthlessness he had displayed with Barbara. Without any apparent concern he exploited Shara's higher emotions, providing the final push that caused her eventually to take her own life.

The Truth Revealed

Brent used his expertise in psychology to telling effect in both relationships. Today, Barbara says: "He knows all the right things to say, all the things a woman wants to hear. He draws women to him."

Most responsible psychologists would have recognized Shara's vulnerability and would not have become involved with her at all, or, if they did pursue a relationship, would have considered her well-being before their self-interest.

Following her suicide, Brent lied to Shara's friends and family, swearing that he had never had a personal or intimate relationship with her, and that he had just been trying to help her.

He did not earn his living as a psychologist (he worked in another profession where his psychology training was useful) and because he did not charge Shara any fee for counseling, no laws were broken. He could easily adopt the role of the good guy in the white doctor's coat and, because he was a skilled deceiver, almost everyone believed him.

The real situation became known only to those who had been closest to Shara, when a scribbled suicide note outlining the true nature of her relationship with Brent was discovered in her apartment, along with many of his personal effects.

People do not conceal the truth unless they feel something needs to be hidden.

That Brent lied suggests he was fully aware that what he had done with Shara was wrong; that he had used his knowledge of psychology to exploit the higher emotions of another, particularly vulnerable, human being.

The Tools of a Rapist

Stranger rapists use physical force or intimidation. Date rapists use a combination of physical force and attraction. Emotional rape involves no physical force.

Emotional rapists rely on subtlety, using a combination of attraction, dishonesty, and manipulation.

If brute force or intimidation was used the victim would become fearful and anxious, likely either to flee or to protect himself (or herself), thereby thwarting the rapist's plans.

Emotional rapists must have the trust or love of their victims—that is the way it works.

As noted earlier, they are usually attractive and/or charismatic characters, nothing like the stereotypical Hollywood villain.

Emotional rapists are usually good at mixing with other people and possess strong social skills.

They can be extremely polite and cultured, but that has no bearing on the fact that they are rapists. (Sexual rapists have been known to ask, so politely, after the event: "Do you mind if I smoke?" Such incongruous good manners do not affect the brutality of the violation.)

Emotional rapists, besides being manipulative and evil, are often passive/active personalities.

That is, they are experts at getting others to act the way they want them to—skilled at finding out how to make a person react in a particular way, and so making things happen without appearing to be responsible.

This last stratagem was evident in the case of Cheryl and Robert, discussed in Chapter 2. When Robert wanted to end the relationship but did not want to appear at fault, he started treating Cheryl extremely badly. It was only her tolerance that forced him to adopt a more provocative plan of action. Most emotional rapists successfully maneuver their victims into taking the desired initiative.

Masters of Disguise—Slaves to Deceit

Those who are evil are masters of disguise; they are not apt to wittingly disclose their true colors— either to others or to themselves.

—Dr. M. Scott Peck, *The People of The Lie*.

In other words, the way people look or act may have little to do with how good or evil they are—and, most importantly, they may not be prepared, or able, to admit their damnable characteristics, even to themselves.

For many, simply being an emotional rapist is so much a part of who they are that they use others naturally, often without forethought or deliberation. Just as good people do the right thing without planning, so the emotional rapist automatically acts in his or her own best interests; the "intent" to exploit another person may be completely subconscious.

For example, when a responsible woman realizes a man has fallen in love with her, she will break off the relationship, or otherwise make sure the true situation is understood, if she does not feel the same way.

In contrast, an emotional rapist instinctively regards such a situation as an opportunity to be exploited to his or her own advantage, whatever that may be (control, power, sex, money, revenge...). Subconsciously the first consideration will often be, "What can I get out of this?"

Questions of Evil

The possibility that some emotional rapists may act subconsciously, without a plan, raises the question of whether or not they should be viewed as evil.

If someone does not have a conscious plan to commit sexual rape or robbery, but does so whenever an opportunity presents itself, that person should, unquestionably, be regarded as evil. The same holds true for the emotional rapist.

Also, it might be argued that rapists behave in ways that even they can neither understand nor control, conceivably because of a childhood relationship with a parent that colored all subsequent relationships. Should they be regarded as evil?

Although conscious intent is absent, the extent of the trauma felt by the victim is the same, regardless of the degree to which the assault, whether sexual or emotional, was planned.

Dr. Scott Peck raises a third possibility in *The People of The Lie*. He argues that all evil is a form of narcissism and is, therefore, a mental illness, as distinct from a spiritual/moral condition.

Ultimately, it is up to each and every one of us to decide whether emotional rapists suffer from mental illness or from a particular spiritual/moral condition, and whether or not they are guilty of evil actions. However, the existence of evil *is* acknowledged here and so the word is used throughout the discussion that follows. Individual readers are free to replace it with the phrase "mentally ill" if they are so inclined.

Acknowledging the existence of evil, and believing that the emotional rapist is the personification of evil, is vitally important if victims are to become survivors.

(This point is discussed in detail in Chapter Five, the first of five chapters dealing with aspects of recovery.)

How Rapists See Themselves

Just as date rapists often do not see their behavior as evil or wrong—some have even been known to ask their victims for another date—the emotional rapist is unlikely to see his or her actions as anything other than socially acceptable behavior.

The parallels with sexual rape go even further. Arguments for the defense in cases of sexual rape often include assertions that the victim in some way got what she deserved; that she "asked for it," in the way she was dressed or acted. The inference is that the rapist only did what the victim wanted, and that the victim was a willing participant.

Emotional rapists offer the same explanation.

People who commit evil do not generally see themselves as bad people. Dale Carnegie, in his classic work *How to Win Friends and Influence People*, goes to great lengths to point out that even the most hardened criminals do not regard themselves as guilty: Al Capone characterized himself as a public benefactor. And since emotional rape is not a crime, an emotional rapist is under even less pressure to admit to any wrongdoing.

Dr. Scott Peck goes further, maintaining that "the evil [ones], deep down, see themselves to be faultless." He suggests that this extreme narcissism in an individual, the idea that he or she can do no wrong, is the root of evil.

Interestingly, the most common denominator of emotional rapists is spiritual arrogance—the belief that they are spiritually superior to almost all others. Most of these beliefs are bolstered by some type of new age or mail-order religions.

More important, a common payoff for the emotional rapist is the feeling of power and control over another person—and to admit guilt or wrongdoing diminishes that feeling of power.

Rape in Other Relationships

The most common form of emotional rape occurs between a man and a woman and uses love. However, rapists, victims, and the emotions used are not limited in form, as the following case studies illustrate...

Rape in the Workplace: John and Peggy

In this case, the higher emotions used were achievement, belonging, trust, and loyalty; the rapist and victim were, respectively, employer and employee.

John worked in a close-knit sales group managed by Peggy, who was extremely good at cultivating a sense of achievement and loyalty to bond her team. She frequently crossed the common boundaries of employer/employee to congratulate certain individuals on a more personal level; praising who they were, instead of their performance.

In this way Peggy developed an almost cult-like sense of loyalty to obtain her payoff, which was control and power. As a member of a cult-like religion, she embraced power as the ultimate goal in life and formally studied principles and techniques that she could use to gain control over others.

These mind-control techniques worked particularly well on John. He said later that there had been a time when, had she asked him to, he would have taken poison for Peggy, an acknowledgment eerily reminiscent of the unquestioning obedience that led to the mass suicide at Jonestown.

John believed whatever Peggy said, even when it contradicted his own judgment or the advice of his trusted friends. After all, she was a high-powered sales executive; successful, attractive, powerful, and charismatic.

Without realizing it, however, he questioned some aspects of Peggy's religion and she immediately turned against him. She even tried to get him fired.

At about the same time, serious irregularities were discovered in Peggy's accounting methods. She had falsified sales records, and her supposed accomplishments were revealed as a total sham when the real figures appeared.

Peggy and the company president, her close friend, were both fired by the board of directors. A co-worker later found written "confessions" in Peggy's desk, admissions that indicated she had been carrying out a hidden agenda, and that she knew what she was doing was wrong.

Unfortunately, before she left the company Peggy was able to damage John's reputation so badly that he, too, was asked to leave. At this point, he was incapable of defending himself because his sense of self-worth had been totally destroyed. He questioned his own judgment about people, feeling he had no reliable tools left to help him cope with life.

John felt as if he had to relearn how to live, from the beginning, and his job memories were so painful that he found he was only able to accept low-paying, temporary work. He turned to alcohol and began to drink to excess, a situation that continued for three years.

However, John did eventually recover, although the process took a long time. He now has a full-time job and is clean and sober. He has finally returned to productive life.

Rape in Time of War: Vietnam

Large institutions are capable of raping multiple victims simultaneously. The Vietnam War is a case in point, one already mentioned in the last chapter.

Few Vietnam veterans who suffered from post-traumatic stress syndrome like to think of themselves as having been raped. However, many admit to feeling used by the United States government.

The higher emotions involved were loyalty, honor, duty, bravery, patriotism, and trust. Those sent to fight trusted the government not to send them into an unjust and unwinnable war, and they trusted the people of the United States to respect the sacrifices they made. Their trust was abused on both counts.

The payoff for the government was an army of young men and women who would kill and die for the administration's hidden political agenda.

The bitterness with which veterans like Raymond recall their wartime experiences is typical: He was just eighteen when he was drafted. He had grown up in an Amish community and did not realize there was any alternative to answering his country's call to arms.

Nearly twenty years later he says: "I did what I thought I was supposed to do; I went and I followed orders. I came home on a stretcher. I was almost crippled, I had nowhere to go, and the people at home didn't exactly welcome us back. I thought then that they should have been spitting on our politicians, not on us."

"We had to do terrible things out there. We were scared out of our minds. The Vietnamese kids we'd give candy bars to during the day would try to blow us up at night. I'm still full of rage when I think about how we were used. We were just kids doing what we were told to do."

More than fifty thousand Americans lost their lives in Vietnam, an appalling total that does not include the large number of drug addicts, alcoholics, and homeless among those who survived to return to their homeland. Many of these cases were caused by post-traumatic rape syndrome, which has remained untreated.

The parents of those who died were also victims of emotional rape. Their sense of patriotism, honor, and duty, which they communicated to their sons and daughters, exerted a powerful influence on their children when the draft papers arrived in the mailbox.

Among those veterans who recall the effects of such parental pressure to serve their country, one telling fact is consistently noted: not a single congressman lost a son or daughter in Vietnam.

The Gulf War, 1991

Governments in all parts of the world, of all political persuasions, have a formidable historical track record of rape and deception of their peoples.

At the end of the 1991 Gulf War, the Iraqi government actually declared that they had defeated the Allied Forces, and for a brief period the people of Iraq believed they had emerged victorious from "The Mother of All Wars," not simply survived "The Mother of All Retreats."

News bulletins vividly captured the spirit of patriotism, loyalty, and trust in their eyes and voices as they celebrated victory. They had no idea that they had been defeated.

Similarly, it seems, the people of the United States and other coalition countries were also skillfully manipulated so that they would give full support to the war effort.

Tales of Iraqi brutality in occupied Kuwait, including particularly shocking stories of sick Kuwaiti babies being tossed out of incubators by the Iraqis, provoked waves of revulsion in the United States. Some time later, however, investigative reporters claimed to have discovered that the incubator stories had been pure fabrication; the invention of a slick public relations firm hired by the Kuwaiti government to galvanize Allied popular opinion in favor of the campaign to liberate Kuwait.

Who are the Victims?

Chapter Two dealt with Cheryl's story, recalling how her boyfriend Robert callously ended their six-year relationship and sent her into a dangerous spiral of depression that almost caused her to take her own life.

But what role did Cheryl play in her own demise? Was she a co-dependent by nature, who sought out someone she could help and care for? To broaden the scope of the question, What roles do the victims of emotional rape play in their fate?

In many instances it appears, with hindsight, that they were at best naïve, at worst foolish. For example, one woman married a man, who turned out to be an emotional rapist, just two months after their first meeting.

However, in considering cases of emotional rape it has to be recognized that the human race covers an incredible range when it comes to the propensity for giving and taking, or for being trusting or suspicious.

At one end of the spectrum are the pure givers; at the other end, the unadulterated takers. The vast majority of people are somewhere in between, striving to maintain value-for-value relationships.

Giving—and Taking

Is emotional rape, then, something that occurs only when a taker meets a giver? Or is it more pervasive than that? Can someone who is in the middle of the spectrum, a person who strives for balance and fairness in relationships, be emotionally raped?

The evidence clearly indicates that all types of people can be vulnerable to emotional rape. It may happen more often to certain personality types, but even people who are normally cautious and careful to protect themselves can be deceived.

Recall Chapter One. Steve knew that Ellen was bankrupt and had a very low income when they married. And he did not exactly throw caution to the wind. Quite the contrary, he took the precaution of drawing up a prenuptial agreement that he believed would protect either of them from having to support the other if the marriage failed.

When the time came to honor the agreement, however, Ellen proved capable of telling outrageous lies about how she had been coerced and misled into signing. Steve was eventually ordered to pay her alimony.

Barbara, one of the subjects of this chapter, was a criminal psychologist who was "street-smart" and trained to be objective and perceptive about a person's true nature. But Brent successfully concealed his dishonesty and hidden agenda from her over an extended period of time. Even when his deceit began to show, hard evidence was required to force her to admit the reality of the situation.

Shifting Responsibility: a Damaging Misconception

Throughout this book parallels have been drawn between sexual date rape and emotional rape. There are significant similarities—and some cannot be overemphasized:

It is misleading and dangerous to believe that date rape or emotional rape only happens to people who are naïve, or who somehow manage to bring this tragedy upon themselves.

That is the very misconception which compounds the trauma of both date rape and emotional rape—and continues to make both forms of rape so easy for the rapist to get away with. Further, it is a misconception which shifts responsibility from the rapist to the victim.

Instead of asking, "Who is responsible?" a more appropriate question is, "What makes it possible for such a broad range of people to be vulnerable to emotional rape?"

What Makes Emotional Rape Possible?

4

Discovery Through Understanding

At the end of Chapter Two we learned how Thelma lost five prime child-bearing years in a relationship that went nowhere. She wanted to get married and have children but her partner Bill had always told her he did not want to start a family. Then he told her he had changed his mind. He *was* ready to enter into both these long-term commitments—but with another woman.

Did Thelma deserve what happened to her? Why didn't she demand more from the relationship? Why didn't she just say no? It could be argued that she got seduced into a bad relationship because she wanted the good things she thought it promised and things just didn't work out.

However, such a conclusion, reached on a very superficial examination of her experience, is not adequate to help us understand the underlying causes of emotional rape, nor to give us a basis for recovery and alert us to ways we might prevent it from happening again.

It must be emphasized: it is not being argued that every relationship that fails is a case of emotional rape.

On the contrary, emotional rape is not the normal way that relationships end, just as date rape is not the usual way that dates end. But both do happen.

Only by understanding what makes emotional rape possible can we address questions of recovery and prevention.

Remember, too, that emotional rape is not limited to love and men/women relationships. It can occur between employer and employee, government and citizen, and in many other situations, so our understanding must include all possible forms.

The Fundamentals

The following three-stage exercise helps to explore the roots of emotional rape—and appreciate why victims can't "Just say no":

1. Try to recall one or two peak experiences in your life, isolated moments when you felt extremely good about yourself. Choose experiences that made you feel the way you would always choose to feel about yourself, given a choice.

2. Try to recall a moment or two when you were exceptionally happy; those moments when you felt as happy as you would like to feel all the time, if you could.

3. Write down just one or two words to remind you of each of those moments.

Your answers help to reveal why people do what they do—and why emotional rape is possible—by identifying what makes us feel good about ourselves and happy with life. Dr. Anthony Walsh, in his book *Human Nature and Love*, notes that all organisms like to feel good about themselves, and that this is a prime-mover of human behavior, the need that ultimately motivates most healthy people.

Analysis of responses to the exercise above, attempting to discern common themes, takes us closer to discovering whether we have command over our own emotional needs. That, in turn, will answer the crucial question of whether we have any power to resist the events and people that seem to fulfill these needs, or to resist the people and institutions that exploit them.

Large groups of people have carried out this exercise, as have many individuals, and the memories they chose as a peak experience or particularly happy moment invariably fitted into one of four broad categories, described by four simple words that encompass most of what makes life worth living:

Achievement, Love, Faith, and Health.

Achievement

The term that most often surfaces is "achievement." Typical examples are winning an athletic competition, creating a successful business, or being selected for a big promotion. Some women said they felt an incredible sense of achievement or fulfillment at the birth of their first child.

(It is the victim's need for achievement, incidentally, which is most often exploited in cases of emotional rape perpetrated by an employer against an employee.)

To better appreciate the raw power of our built-in need for achievement, consider that it may be fueling one of the biggest drug problems facing our society today.

Cocaine, users commonly explain, makes them feel as if they have just accomplished something, or done something, extremely well. In other words, using cocaine produces a feeling of achievement. Is it any wonder that such a substance, one that simulates the number-one peak experience in life, has become one of our most serious problem drugs.

Unlike the reaction to cocaine, however, the feeling of achievement identified as a peak experience by those completing our test nearly always involved something they had to work hard for; no one identified a lucky win as a peak experience. Apparently, it is not winning, *per se*, that is important.

Likewise, no drug-induced feeling of achievement was recalled as a peak experience.

It is the attainment of a goal that is worked for and earned which is most memorable to most people.

A sense of accomplishment, it seems, is one of the best feelings a person can have.

Love

Next to achievement, the word most commonly used to describe peak experiences is "love." Giving and receiving love makes us feel good about ourselves and others, and creates a feeling of happiness.

Of course, recognizing the importance of love in our lives is certainly no new discovery.

In *Human Nature and Love,* Dr. Walsh writes: "Love is the noblest, most beautiful, inspiring, exquisite, ecstatic, and meaningful experience of humanity."

The respected Jewish psychiatrist, Victor Frankl, a survivor of four Nazi death camps and author of *Man's Search For Meaning,* says: "Love is the ultimate and the highest goal to which man can aspire."

They are referring to real love—not erotic or romantic love, nor sex, but real love. And real love is as real love does.

To love someone is not only to share yourself, but also to "do" for them; whether that is just taking out the garbage, or nursing them through an illness.

It doesn't matter how many times one person says

**to another "I love you," the words cannot refer to real
love if that person's actions are always in his or her
own best interests.**

- True love for others is wanting to help them fulfill every
one of their needs.
- If they need to achieve a particular goal to feel good
about themselves, your natural reaction is to help.
- If they suffer from an illness or disease, you want to
nurse them back to health.
- You want to provide the freedom and space that will enable them to find meaning and purpose in life, through
whatever form of faith they believe in. When they cannot
believe in themselves, you believe in them until their
sense of self-worth returns.

Faith

One woman identified her peak experience as the way she
felt after an intensive spiritual retreat. She said she felt total acceptance and love, not only from God, but from everyone there. "It was wonderful," she recalled.

Her peak experience involved faith—one of the less frequently recalled of our four categories, but nonetheless a
significant one.

Other faith-related, or spiritual, peaks include near-
death experiences, when people reported having seen a
white light and having felt the unconditional love of God.

**This book accepts an expansive definition of faith,
a definition that encompasses "the primary force causing man to search for an ultimate meaning and purpose in life."**

This ultimate meaning exceeds man's finite intellectual
capabilities. Victor Frankl identifies it as a "supra-mean-
ing." Drawing upon his experiences in the concentration
camps, Frankl recalls that prisoners who lost faith in the

meaning and purpose of their lives were doomed. That purpose itself does not have to be grandiose.

In his case, Frankl saw himself lecturing and writing on what he had learned about human nature during the time he was imprisoned. His vision of his own meaning and purpose preserved his will to live, despite such terrible circumstances.

Belief in the future is one of the best ways to survive periods of extreme hardship.

Health

Health is the least commonly recalled category of peak experiences or happiness. People usually referred to health if they had recovered from a debilitating illness, or had been cured of a potentially fatal disease.

For example, one man who was treated for a serious cancer thought he was going to die, until he learned the cancerous growth had been successfully removed.

He identified the moment his doctor told him that he was going to live as one of his peak experiences.

The definition of health used here is also a broad one, including most of the things we consider necessary for our physical well-being: physical safety and security, shelter, food, water, oxygen, and our biological need for sex.

The Four Basic Ingredients

There are four basic "ingredients" that together make emotional rape possible:

■ The **first** of these encompasses the peak-experience categories—Health, Achievement, Love, and Faith—that we discussed above. These can be brought together in the acronym HALF. (It is a playful, if usefully memorable, acronym, because if you have HALF, you have ALL you need.)

■ The **second** is Powerlessness. We are powerless in the face of our need for the HALF factors, and therefore vulnerable to emotional rapists who are skilled at creating the illusion that they are in some way satisfying one or more of these needs.

■ The **third** is the basic human tendency to believe *as* true what we wish *was* true—often despite apparently strong evidence to the contrary. The "bad-call bias" analogy, outlined later, helps us better understand this tendency.

■ The **fourth** and final ingredient is evil—acknowledging that evil exists in the world and that the actions of emotional rapists are a form of malignant narcissism, otherwise defined as evil.

Each of these is worthy of detailed examination...

The HALF Factors

Nearly all our emotions and needs relate to one or more of the HALF factors—Health, Achievement, Love, and Faith.

For example, patriotism, loyalty, trust, and friendship are forms and shades of love. Anger can be viewed as love turned inside out. Fear suggests faith or a belief in a negative outcome. Success relates to achievement; failure is the other side of achievement...And so on.

The notion that people are primarily motivated by higher emotions, the HALF factors, as opposed to lower ones, or deficiencies, is consistent with the teachings of the psychiatrist and scholar Abraham Maslow.

In *Toward a Psychology of Being,* he identifies four basic human needs of life: safety and security, belonging and affection, respect and self-respect, and self-actualization. These have clear similarities to health, love, and achievement, although he does not identify any factors that are obviously related to spiritual belief or faith.

Those who have doubts about the universal nature of the HALF factors would find themselves convinced after testing the responses of others to the exercise set out at the start of this chapter.

Ask people to answer those questions about peak experiences and happiness, their answers will all fall naturally into one of the HALF factor categories.

Emotional rapists are able to create the illusion that they are fulfilling one or more of these HALF factors—the illusion that they are satisfying a basic and compelling need in the lives of their prey.

Powerlessness

Whatever god we believe in, whatever explanation for the creation of the universe we find acceptable, one certainty is that humankind had no say in the fundamental laws governing man's condition.

Like it or not, our basic needs are built-in, unchangeable, and we are powerless to resist them.

However, to intellectualize about human needs is quite different, on a very important basic level, from experiencing them.

To intellectualize about the need for oxygen is not the same as gasping for breath when it isn't there; to gasp is truly to appreciate the need for oxygen, at a deeper level. In normal life, we simply take it for granted, rarely having to think about how powerless we are in its absence.

Similarly, we have to be fully aware of our powerlessness in the face of the HALF factors (Health, Achievement, Love, and Faith).

Our need for sex affords perhaps the best illustration of that powerlessness. Consider that young children, yet to experience the potent hormonal changes of puberty, generally see sex as disgusting or amusing, not compelling.

This attitude changes, however, with the arrival of adulthood, when those hormones exert their influence. But it takes a rare combination of intelligence, objectivity and courage for an individual to see that he or she is truly powerless over their attraction to the opposite sex (or to the same sex, in some instances); that it really isn't their idea.

Such basic needs, in most cases, are not visible—we can't see health, achievement, love, or faith—but we can surely see their effects, both positive, when they are in bloom, and negative, when they are thwarted.

Easy Prey: Our Need for Health

It is easy to understand how someone could be raped by a person willing to prey on the built-in need for health.

Most people will go to any lengths to survive; we have a built-in survival instinct. Anyone who was able to convince a person with a terminal illness that there was a magic cure could surely strip that sick person, perhaps the entire family, of almost everything they owned.

In the same way, if you had a cure for AIDS you could use that cure to become an extremely wealthy and powerful person.

This in itself, of course, would not constitute emotional rape. Anyone who possessed such a cure would be entitled to whatever rewards the market would bear. However, anyone who did not have any cure but misled AIDS sufferers into believing that he did, to profit financially or in some other way, would be guilty of emotional rape.

Likewise, a doctor or hospital whose main objective is to squeeze every last penny out of a patient (or their insurance company), rather than being primarily concerned for the well-being of the patient, is committing emotional rape.

In such cases, many of which have been well documented, our trust, and need for health, are being exploited.

Most of us trust in the skill and integrity of our physicians. We have to believe they have our best interests at heart and are not simply covetous of our money.

Fortunately, the majority of physicians are worthy of such trust. Unfortunately, there are exceptions.

Easy Prey:
Our Needs to Achieve, Love and Have Faith

It is not as easy to comprehend our powerlessness to resist the need to achieve, love, and have faith. We like to believe we have control in these areas of life.

However, our lack of control over these other three HALF factors is as complete as it is in concerns of health.

If anything, it is more complete, which is why people select achievement, love, and faith as their peak experiences more often than they select health. It is also why people choose to jeopardize their health by injecting, swallowing or inhaling highly toxic, addictive substances to simulate the feelings of achievement and love.

The human need for faith was the HALF factor exploited by those unscrupulous "televangelists" whose vigorous TV sermons inspired thousands to part with their hard-earned money, as gifts for the tele-ministries. This exploitation rightly earned some such preachers long prison terms.

In *When All You've Ever Wanted Isn't Enough,* Harold Kushner describes our built-in need for faith as an insatiable hunger for meaning and significance, planted by God. Victor Frankl argues convincingly that striving to find a meaning in one's life, the search for faith, is the primary motivational force in man.

Accepting our powerlessness in the face of the HALF factors enables us to see what makes emotional rape possible.

Add to that the need felt by most people to *give* love, and to *work* for achievement, and the reasons for our vulnerability to emotional rape become clear.

(It is difficult to imagine a totally self-centered person being emotionally raped. Their narcissism or greed might blind them to reality, but that would not, by our definition, lead to emotional rape. Emotional rape is defined as the use of a *higher* emotion—not a lower emotion—without consent.)

We must not underestimate the importance of understanding powerlessness.

Paradoxically, recognizing powerlessness is a very powerful step forward for the emotional rape victim, one of the first steps towards regaining some degree of control over his or her life.

Like a sailor on the ocean, we do not have the ability to navigate an ideal course through life. We cannot control the basic elements, the winds and currents.

However, once we accept this lack of control we can choose to steer clear of certain conditions. We can recognize when those conditions are right for emotional rape—and avoid taking unnecessary risks.

The Bad-Call Bias

Anyone who plays tennis has experienced the "bad-call bias." The ball hits a line and one player sees it as out while the other player is certain it was in.

Why is it in such cases that each player usually sees the ball as having dropped in their own favor? Are they all cheats? The explanation is simple: what we perceive is influenced by what we want to believe. We want to believe that the person we love also loves us, that we are worthy of love and achievement, and that the people we trust are worthy of our trust.

Robert Ringer, author of *Looking Out For #1*, makes the point with crystal clarity in his book *Living Without Limits*: **"We don't love the truth, but we want to make true what we love."**

In relationships, we interpret the behavior of the ones we love or trust to match our own needs—our desire to see what we want to see distorts our good judgment.

Our powerlessness in the face of our built-in needs for love and achievement, combined with this tendency to believe what we want to believe, makes almost everyone susceptible to emotional rape.

Evil: the Final Ingredient

Thus far we have identified the HALF needs—Health, Achievement, Love, and Faith—our powerlessness in the face of these needs, and the natural tendency to distort our good judgment to see what we want to believe. These are important considerations to help answer the central question of this chapter: What makes emotional rape possible?

However, our list of answers is incomplete. In all cases something else is present, a final ingredient that can only be adequately identified as evil.

As noted in Chapter Three, Dr. Peck, in *The People of The Lie*, takes the position that evil is a form of malignant narcissism, a narcissism that goes far beyond the dictionary definition of "love of one's own body."

Malignant narcissism is total self-absorption. People who are evil put their own self-interest and desires before all else, unlike mentally healthy adults who, as Dr. Peck points out, submit themselves to some higher power or ideal, such as God, truth, love, honesty, or fairness. Evil people seemingly lack the ability to do this. There is also an element of laziness in evil. It takes work to grow spiritually, and evil people are not willing to make that effort.

Another description of evil might be malignant *laziness* **and narcissism.**

Selfish Exploitation

Our need for sex is built-in and good, as well as essential for the survival of the human species. The evil act of sexual rape occurs when a man places his own narcissistic needs for power and control above all else.

Our higher emotions and needs for health, achievement, love, and faith—the HALF factors—are built-in and good. But emotional rape takes place when a lazy, narcissistic human being puts his or her own vested interests and desires before the notions of goodness, fairness and honesty.

For example, Ellen, who emotionally raped Steve, put her narcissistic need for her acting career above the sanctity of love.

Brent, who emotionally raped Barbara and pushed Shara into suicide, placed his narcissistic need for sex and power over women above human compassion, decency, even the ethics of his professional training.

Furthermore, we know that both Ellen and Brent were in some way conscious of their ill-intent because they both lied about their actions.

Ellen denied having a hidden agenda, although Steve had found her diary in which she detailed all her secret personal ambitions.

After Shara's suicide Brent lied to her friends and family about the nature of his relationship with her.

A person does not lie unless they are aware that something needs hiding.

The Antithesis of Life

If the HALF factors (Health, Achievement, Love, and Faith) represent goodness, then those acts and deeds that take away those factors are evil. Any action that unfairly interferes with someone else's pursuit of HALF is evil.

Evil goes against life—quite appropriately it is "live" spelled backwards. Dr. Peck defines evil as "that force... that seeks to kill life or liveliness. And goodness is the opposite. Goodness is that which promotes life and liveliness."

What could promote life and liveliness more than Health, Achievement, Love, and Faith? Conversely, what human acts can interfere with the HALF factors more than emotional rape?

Victor Frankl writes that "There are really only two races in the world, the decent race and the indecent race, and that both races penetrate into all groups of society."

One of evil's higher accomplishments has been to convince many of "the decent race" that it doesn't exist; putting those good people off their guard, and making them even more vulnerable.

Recognizing that evil exists, and understanding its role in emotional rape, is vital to recovery and prevention.

Do Victims Deserve It?

Consider again the opening questions of this chapter: Did Thelma deserve what happened to her? Why didn't she just say no to a relationship that was going nowhere?

It should now be clear that saying no to emotional rape just isn't that simple. It is saying no to something that controls your needs, thoughts, and perceptions.

People should not feel foolish or weak if their needs for one or more of the HALF factors (Health, Achievement, Love, and Faith) caused some temporary blindness of their good judgment. Even the best scientists, who are trained to observe and think rationally, have occasionally succumbed to this need to distort reality.

For example, the "discovery" of cold fusion once made front-page headlines.

If the story was true it meant that the same nuclear reactions that release the enormous amounts of energy in the sun could be contained and controlled in a small jar, hence this major scientific breakthrough was quickly dubbed "fusion in a jar."

The "discovery" was always controversial, however, and the scientific community eventually determined it was a mistake, prompting the Public Broadcasting Service to produce a television special on the saga, called, appropriately, *ConFusion in a Jar.*

The researchers' powerlessness in the face of their need for achievement, combined with their desire to see only what they wanted to see, was behind the error. The need for achievement affected not only what the scientists chose to believe, but how they interpreted what they perceived.

Rather than lying intentionally, to mislead the public or the media, the researchers simply saw what they longed to see.

This example demonstrates an alarming truth: unless we are constantly vigilant, "bad-call bias" is always liable to influence good judgment.

If scientists can be subject to this tendency to distort the truth, then it can surely happen to the average unsuspecting person.

The 'Unfair' Qualification

What makes emotional rape possible is a combination of powerlessness and distortion. We are powerless in the face of our instinctive needs for the HALF factors (Health,

Achievement, Love, and Faith), and our built-in bias towards seeing what we want to see distorts our judgment.

Rapists exploit this situation, unfairly using our natural human instincts and limitations for personal gain or gratification.

The word "unfair" is a significant qualifier here. In our daily relationships we cannot avoid using, in some way, the powerlessness of others in the face of the HALF factors. For example, we reward our spouses with embraces of love, and praise for achievement, when they do something that fulfills our own needs, and we try to appeal to our associates' need for achievement to persuade them to join us in a business venture.

When these interactions occur honestly, in an equal value-for-value exchange between individuals, they enhance life and advance both the individual and society. Orchestrated unfairly, however, they result in human tragedy.

It is only the vital human qualities of responsibility, honesty, and a sense of fair play that keep fraud, crime, and rape from being the normal way of life.

The degree to which individuals are powerless in the face of the different HALF factors will vary. Some people may be capable of keeping in check their need for love but not their need for achievement.

However, we can all expect to be as powerless in the face of some HALF factors as drug addicts are powerless to resist addictive drugs.

Not that the needs for achievement, love, health and faith are addictions in the normal sense of that word. They are natural gifts that make life worth living, and it is the misuse of these gifts that is wrong; not the gifts themselves, or our powerlessness to control them.

Furthermore, unlike addiction, satisfying a HALF need does not usually increase the power of that need. Only on rare occasions does this happen; for example, when the career high-achiever becomes a workaholic.

Why HALF?

Why do we need the HALF factors (Health, Achievement, Love, and Faith)? Why do we not need other factors, perhaps some for which we do not even have names? By what rules do we say that the HALF factors are good, and that anything that unfairly interferes with HALF is evil?

Why does any of this matter?

■ First, understanding the HALF factors matters to emotional rape victims because HALF is one-fourth of what makes emotional rape possible, and hence is one fourth of the basis for recovery and prevention.

■ Second, another one-fourth, the difficult notion of powerlessness, is impossible to comprehend if the HALF factors are not accepted as basic human needs.

We can readily establish that we are powerless to resist the HALF factors by trying to imagine life without health, achievement, love or faith—by going to extremes, an exercise that also illustrates how evil, the last of the four emotional rape ingredients, is the antithesis of life.

Extreme Alternatives

Imagine a world in which the HALF factors (Health, Achievement, Love, and Faith) were totally absent; a non-HALF world, a life with no built-in desires for health, achievement, love, or faith. Such an existence would, indeed, be without purpose, and it is doubtful whether the human species as we know it would survive.

This is not a hypothetical deduction. We know that the consistent abuse of a person's built-in need for the HALF factors can lead to depression and suicide. Shara, who killed herself by jumping off a freeway overpass, was such a person.

Human beings cannot exist without love. Man is one of

the few mammals whose offspring are not equipped for survival on their own. Human babies remain dependent upon others for a long time, longer than many other species. Without the love and care of the parent for the child, how many of us could have survived alone?

Even if the physical necessities (food, water, clothing and shelter) are provided, the absence of love and affection has lasting negative consequences, both emotional and physical, on young children.

We can take our inquiry a step further by replacing positive with negative, by trying to visualize a world in which the opposites of the HALF factors—disease, destruction, hate, and nihilism—determine our built-in desires. Such a world would not survive for long.

Disregarding the obvious destructive effects of disease, it would be a world in which every man and woman would function and act solely for himself or herself: no one would love or care for anyone else; cooperation would be nonexistent; no one would build or create.

In this hypothetical anti-HALF world, there would be nothing to restrain people from killing and plundering to satisfy their daily needs for money or food. Crime would reach epidemic proportions. Indeed, no one would believe crime was wrong in such a world, so such behavior would not be considered criminal. An orgy of self-destruction would extinguish human life as we know it. An anti-HALF world, a totally evil world, simply would not last.

Evil is wrong because it does not work, and most of us have a built-in sense of what is right and wrong; it is not a lesson we can afford to learn by trial and error.

The Lessons of History

Throughout history there have been occasions when various forms and degrees of anti-HALF behavior became the acceptable norm.

A recent example occurred in the aftermath of the Gulf War, when Iraq became a battleground for various Iraqi factions who hoped to overthrow Saddam Hussein. The cost in human life to the country was greater than that incurred during the confrontation with the coalition forces; thousands of innocent civilians died and huge tracts of land were devastated.

This additional destruction was caused by one group killing and plundering another to gain control and ensure survival.

When such a situation occurs on a group level, the destruction usually stops when one faction is victorious. Perpetrated on an individual level, however, it would continue until only one person remained.

Communism furnishes us with an example of what happens in a society that thwarts the HALF factor of achievement. Decisions made at a bureaucratic level about who will, and who will not, be allowed to achieve or profit smother the natural forces that motivate individuals. For an economic system to compete on a global basis, everyone in that system has to have an opportunity to achieve success through their own efforts.

Society's Survival Instinct

The HALF factors (Health, Achievement, Love, and Faith) are necessary for the survival of human life as we know it. **Though we like to think we each have a choice about what our needs are, we can tolerate only a minimal amount of anti-HALF or non-HALF behavior without causing great harm to mankind.**

Perhaps that is why the HALF factors are so powerful and so much a part of human nature. Just as the built-in need for sex is essential for the continued survival of the human species, the HALF factors are essential to the survival of any complex society that builds and creates.

Towards Recovery

Past responses to the questions posed at the beginning of this chapter suggest that the peak experiences and happiest moments recalled most often are those involving achievement and love.

Frequently, we associate our peak experiences with achievement and our happiest moments with love.

Large institutions have exploited the need for achievement in many cases of emotional rape, however our need for love, commonly in one-on-one relationships, is the need most frequently abused.

This need is incredibly powerful.

In his book *The Art of Loving,* Erich Fromm notes that man is keenly aware of his innate aloneness and separateness, and that he would go insane if he couldn't unite himself, in some way, with another being.

Fromm says this intense "desire for interpersonal fusion is the most powerful striving in man," and that it is possible only when two beings "communicate with each other from the center of their existence."

In other words, when you love someone, you put your soul in their hands. That is the essence of real love—sharing yourself, your soul, with another being—and honesty and openness are essential.

You cannot share the real "you" if you are dishonest about who "you" are (then the relationship will be built on deception, not love). Herein lies the enormous destructive capability of emotional rape. When people give of themselves at the level of real love and then have that gift exploited by another, it becomes extremely difficult for them to share themselves again.

Recovering and rebuilding the ability to love and trust is a monumental task when something as sacred as real love is abused—but it is possible.

Recovery:
Believe it Will Happen 5

The Language of Healing

To transform tragedy into unique recovery it is essential
that the victim of emotional rape understands exactly
what has happened and participates fully in his, or her,
own healing process. However, until now there has been
no clinical term for emotional rape, so there is no established terminology available.

Discussing the process of healing means importing an
unfamiliar mixture of terminologies, using a vocabulary
more commonly employed to describe recovery from sexual
rape and other emotional traumas, including death,
physical victimization or the loss of a loved one

It is a borrowed vocabulary that draws on the language
of medicine and psychology, emotional experience and
spiritual ideas.

This is a logical and necessary mixture because, as we
saw in the last chapter, the underlying basis for emotional
rape is man's inherent powerlessness over the HALF factors—which themselves encompass qualities that are
medical (Health), psychological (Achievement), emotional
(Love), and spiritual (Faith).

This chapter focuses on faith—on believing that it is possible to recover. It is the first of five chapters dealing with recovery.

We shall see that the healing process can result in an amazing metamorphosis. In fact, we have reached the point where victims can begin to see themselves as survivors.

Faith is not necessarily linked to religion. It is simply the belief that you will recover, the belief in your own magnificence, the belief that there is more to life than is immediately obvious.

Having faith that there is meaning and purpose to life and to suffering helps to open the doors to a full recovery.

Accept Your Transformation

Victims may find it difficult to believe but emotional rape is not the end of the world. It can be a growing experience—a painful experience, but nonetheless an opportunity for personal growth. Recognizing its possibilities moves victims closer to their own transformation.

Consider how a caterpillar must struggle to break free of the cocoon before it becomes a butterfly, a thing of beauty and flight. That butterfly will die if the cocoon is slit open to make it easier to emerge. For reasons that we do not fully understand, the struggle is necessary for the butterfly's survival and transformation.

The same principle applies to many areas of human experience: we must all struggle before we are transformed into a more beautiful expression of ourselves.

In the aftermath of emotional rape the victim may feel incredibly alone and ponder deeply upon the meaning and purpose of life. But he or she will emerge from this struggle as a better, more complete individual.

Emergency Support

When you are trying to recover from emotional rape, your sustaining triangle of health, achievement, and love—the framework of your wholeness—has been badly damaged.

One of those three life-supporting HALF factors, abused in the act of rape, is in need of restoration. And it is faith, the fourth, all-important HALF factor, that we rely upon to shore up the structure, to replace the missing factor until it is repaired.

Without faith, as the drawing above suggests, this life-sustaining triangle can collapse because one of the three sides is damaged.

When someone loses their job, their means to achievement, it can affect their love relationships. The stresses arising from the lack of achievement and love then begin to affect physical health. Before long the whole triangle is endangered.

We should not underestimate the importance of faith in this "emergency and recovery" role—the importance of knowing that the triangle *will* be restored, even though it may take some time, and that, just possibly, something positive will emerge from all the pain.

Suffering and Growth

If you face a problem, whether you are able to solve it or not, you will grow.
—Dr. Elisabeth Kubler-Ross, *Death—The Final Stage of Growth.*

The knowledge that others have recovered from emotional rape and from many more severe crises can strengthen your faith.

Dr. Kubler-Ross, a psychiatrist and authority on death and dying, studied the personal stories of people confronting their own deaths and concluded that facing any tragedy means "facing the ultimate question of the meaning of life." She reminds us that:

"If we really want to live, we must have the courage to recognize that life is ultimately very short and that everything we do counts."

Although emotional rape may be the most underrated traumatic experience of our day, it is not the worst—other individuals have suffered greater trauma and survived.

Dr. Victor Frankl, a concentration camp survivor who was quoted earlier in this book, offers this thought:

"To live is to suffer, to survive is to find meaning in the suffering."

What do death camps have to do with our inquiry? After all, the physical realities of concentration camps are not present in emotional rape. In fact, the comparison is illuminating.

Only someone who has lived through the aftermath of emotional rape can appreciate the degree of mental anguish endured by the victim. And non-physical suffering can be very intense, often just as severe, if not worse, than physical pain.

Dr. Frankl makes this point, describing how a camp guard clubbed him over the head for no reason. He recalls that he experienced less trauma from the physical pain than from the "injustice of it all." Even while enduring the terrible material hardships of a concentration camp, his emotional pain was, at times, harder to bear than his physical suffering.

Spiritual Faith

There is another aspect of faith that is vital to recovery:

- The belief that there is more to life than our everyday, readily apparent existence...
- The belief that there is a Greater Power, an Intelligence, a Creative Force—your god—which gives a greater significance to the human condition...
- The belief that when posing the question, Is this all there is? the answer is definitely, No.

For victims of emotional rape, believing that answer is always going to be difficult. Amid the trauma, all-there-is will almost certainly not look all-that-good. Most will have had their basic belief in life shattered, and will need to hold on to something tangible that tells them there is a meaning and purpose to life.

It bears repeating that this aspect of faith does not have to be linked to religious belief, although it's fine if it is. Science and simple observation, as opposed to religion, convinced me at the very root of my being that, put simply, there is more to life than meets the eye.

Inexplicable Observations

My own observation occurred when my sister, who lives in Chicago, visited me at my home in California.

She told me how she had dreamed about our father the night before. He was retired and lived in Florida, but my sister, who had had no recent contact with our father, remembered vividly that in her dream he had been much closer, just up the west coast in San Francisco. She also clearly remembered that he had been extremely sad.

That evening, after my sister had left, the phone rang and it was my father. He was calling from San Francisco, and he was very sad. His last living brother had died suddenly and my father had traveled from Florida to help with the funeral arrangements.

My sister's dream had been uncannily, inexplicably accurate, and the circumstances were such that it could not be dismissed as mere coincidence. The incident demonstrated to me, firsthand, the reality of greater powers beyond our comprehension, powers that give our lives greater significance and meaning.

I have heard of many other, similar examples. Indeed, one occurred during the investigation into the so-called "Hillside Strangler" murders in California.

A German psychic traveled all the way to Los Angeles at his own expense and told police he had dreamed that two Italians, both aged about thirty-five, were responsible for the killings. His dream, too, proved correct. Two Italian-Americans, relatives, with an average age of about thirty-five, were eventually found guilty of the murders.

Because emotional rape can leave a person devastated, it sometimes destroys the belief that anything really matters. That must not happen.

Your belief system may have been turned upside-down, and that in itself is traumatic, however the significant lesson of the examples above, and innumerable similar instances that have occurred to other people, is that there is much more to life than we can readily understand.

Many survivors of emotional rape say that appreciating the inexplicable complexity of life played a vital part in their recovery—they had a belief in the intangible that gave them something to hold on to.

Science and Belief

Many survivors also recall a need to hold on to something tangible, so they can continue believing that what they do, the decisions they make and how they live their lives, really counts. The discoveries of modern science can provide that tangible lifeline.

Historically, the scientific method was devoted to applying reason and logic in the examination of all things and was generally regarded as totally incompatible with faith or belief. The rationalist science of yesteryear held that life was not created by some Greater Power or Intelligence.

It was believed instead that chemicals in the atmosphere were hit by lightning billions of years ago and formed amino acids. These in turn reacted to form proteins that somehow came together to start life.

This theory reduces human beings to little more than products of out-of-control chemical reactions. If it is true, then nothing has any purpose, and therefore the pain we experience is meaningless.

(It is a theory that may suit the emotional rapist, but for the victim it is a painful thought, one that inevitably leads to doubts about whether life is worth living.)

Today, however, science is offering the most compelling evidence that this "lightning strike" theory of creation is totally unrealistic. In their book *Evolution from Space*, the two respected astrophysicists Sir Fred Hoyle and N. C. Wickramasinghe present compelling scientific arguments showing that the probability of the spontaneous emergence of life from random chemical reactions is as close to zero as can be imagined.

Increasingly, scientists agree that even the most basic element of life, the cell, is so incredibly complex that it is illogical and unreasonable to suggest such an amazing structure was a chance creation.

From this position, the argument for the existence of

an Intelligence, a Creative Force—that which some people call God—becomes increasingly difficult to ignore. Some things simply cannot be explained any other way.

Modern scientific thinking upholds the very real possibility that everything we do, every decision we make, does have a place in a greater universal scheme...the possibility that our lives really do matter and that suffering (the suffering of a victim of emotional rape, for example) really matters.

The Life Beyond

Furthermore, there is now overwhelming evidence that life does not end after death. Such evidence has been gained by studying the cases of people who have died and been returned to life, a phenomenon referred to as a "near-death experience" (NDE).

Dr. Raymond Moody Jr., a medical doctor who has spent a large portion of his career studying NDEs, deals convincingly with this subject in his book, *The Light Beyond.*

Dr. Moody cites the case of one woman who had such an experience and was later able to describe to the doctor the procedures and medical instruments he had used to resuscitate her, right down to their colors. A skeptic might argue that she must simply have been conscious throughout the experience; that she saw what occurred, perhaps through peripheral vision. However, such an explanation wasn't plausible—the woman had been blind for over fifty years.

Significantly, many people who have had a NDE report having experienced every good and bad effect their life had on others, as if they were the others. They returned to life with the clear and consistent message that love and knowledge are the only real values in life.

Acknowledge What Happened

We have already mentioned how, even while facing the horrors of the concentration camps, Dr. Frankl realized the importance of acknowledging the truth about what was happening to him.

Fellow prisoners who regarded their lives as unreal, or who tried to shut out the reality and live in the past, found their lives became meaningless and their survival less likely. Denying the reality of the situation denied them the opportunity to challenge their hardships and to test their inner strength.

Paradoxically, acknowledging that (as prisoners) they were victims, and that their daily lives were full of suffering, was an important part of survival.

There are many paradoxes on the road to recovery from emotional rape. Healing is not instantaneous, it takes time—and denying what happened only prolongs the process.

Denial takes many forms, including self-blame. As we saw in Chapter Two, friends, family, even counselors, may encourage this feeling, asking questions about the victim's past, even his or her early childhood. Such questions shift the blame for what happened from the rapist to the victim.

It is of course possible that a negative childhood experience, such as sexual abuse, could exacerbate the trauma of sexual rape in adulthood.

Likewise, whether the rape is sexual or emotional, a therapist may need to help the victim come to terms with a related traumatic experience from his or her childhood, in conjunction with the recent trauma.

However, even when this is the case and such childhood experiences are present, that does not make the person who was raped responsible for what happened. Those experiences are simply other evil acts which the victim was subject to and must deal with in later life.

Victims of sexual rape, particularly date rape, often

blame themselves, asking questions like, "I made the wrong choice in who to date. What is wrong with my judgment? What is wrong with me?"

This is nonsense. Rape is caused by the rapist—not by the person who is raped.

As a means to recovery, denial is useless. A more productive approach is the one proposed by Dr. Frankl: acknowledge that you have come face to face with evil and accept the inner challenge which follows from that acknowledgment.

Acknowledge the Existence of Evil

There really are people, and institutions made up of people, who respond with hatred in the presence of goodness and would destroy the good insofar as it is their power to do so. They do this not with conscious malice but blindly, lacking awareness of their own evil, indeed, seeking to avoid any such awareness. Evil people hate the light because it reveals themselves to themselves. They hate goodness because it reveals their badness; they hate love because it reveals their laziness. They will destroy the light, the goodness, the love, in order to avoid the pain of such self-awareness.

—Dr. M. Scott Peck, *The Road Less Traveled.*

This is the reality, stated in just a few short words: evil does exist. However, we must realize that it seldom looks like the monsters and villains beloved of Hollywood films, or wears uniforms that epitomize evil, like those of the Gestapo of Nazi Germany.

Recall how Dr. Jeffrey MacDonald, a Princeton-educated physician, appeared so attractive, intelligent, and charismatic that he was interviewed on a television talk show about the brutal murders of his pregnant wife and two small children in their own home. He was later charged with the crime in a chilling case. He was found guilty of killing his entire family with an ice pick and club.

Attractive, intelligent people are as capable of evil as those who are ugly or deformed—arguably more so. Charm can be used as a key to open many doors, not always with good intentions.

Victims of emotional rape are not responsible for the evil that befell them. They are responsible only for the choices *they* make between good and evil, not the choices other people make. They did not deserve what happened to them, any more than Dr. MacDonald's family deserved to be murdered in their beds.

Bad Things Do Happen to Good People

God is all powerful.
God is all good.
Terrible things happen.

Theologian Frederick Buechner shrewdly observed that you can match any two of these three propositions, but never all three.

(The propositions referred specifically to God, so we will do the same throughout this section. However, the words Creative Force, Intelligence, or Greater Power can be substituted. The logical argument remains the same.)

It is a fact that terrible things, like emotional rape, do sometimes happen to people who have been good, kind, generous and loving. And it is also a fact that many of us believe in the notion that neither good nor bad things happen without purpose or meaning.

So, even when something happens that appears to be unfair and unjust, we often assume that the victim must have done something to deserve the misfortune.

The underlying assumption is that there is a god who is all powerful, all good and controls everything. This assumption, as the dilemma of our three propositions reminds us, is plainly a problem.

One obvious solution, a simple one, is to accept that God is not all powerful. This proposition still accepts God as the creator of everything and allows Him to remain all good, but it also admits that terrible things do happen to good people, a truth we cannot deny.

Perhaps the one limitation God faced in creating the universe was that nothing could be created without its opposite.

If positively charged particles, protons, were created, then an equal number of negatively charged particles, electrons, also had to exist. For every positive emotion there had to be a balancing negative one. As soon as good was created there was also evil—and then the power to choose was introduced into this world of alternatives.

If freedom of choice was impossible and all human actions were controlled by a Greater Power, human beings would be reduced to the status of robots, just as we are in the "lightning strike" theory of creation, with no meaning or purpose. We would not be human.

Life is all about the choices we make, and we cannot be free to choose good unless we are also free to choose evil.

Would life without this freedom to choose between good and evil be better? Would love be as fulfilling without hate? Would achievement be as exhilarating without failure?

Because we have the freedom to choose between good and evil, and because we do not live forever, every moment of our lives, every decision we make, counts.

Life is not about winning or losing, but discovering who we really are—about love and knowledge. How could we discover who we are, or learn about love and knowledge, in a world with no opposites, no chance of failure, no ability to choose?

Bad things *do* happen to good people, but that doesn't mean those people must therefore be bad, or otherwise deserving of misfortune. It is simply that those good people are the victims, thence survivors, of choices that are made; sometimes their own choices, sometimes the choices of others.

Accept Your Own Magnificence

The victims of evil do not escape responsibility altogether.

Although they were not to blame for what happened, they do have a responsibility for their own recovery. They have to be willing to recover. Not to force the process, just willing to be willing, and to accept the power to do what they have to do.

They must not underestimate their own magnificence.

Just because we might not have any idea how a wound heals itself doesn't prevent the process from taking its course. Commonsense and experience tell us that simple measures—keeping the wound clean and taking good care of ourselves—will help (Chapter Seven offers practical advice on physical well-being during recovery).

Being willing to recover is simply making sure that you are not standing in your own way, or otherwise interfering with the healing process.

Remember, too, that emotional rape may turn out to be one of the best things that has happened to you, although this will seem unlikely while you are still suffering from the traumatic aftermath. Such life-altering experiences send powerful warnings that something in life—yours, mine, or anyone's—is not right.

Many people who have suffered minor heart attacks later credit those unwelcome occurrences with saving their lives, causing them to modify their lifestyle, become more aware of their bodies; in short, to be transformed.

Survivors of emotional rape can have a new and better life, and the emotional strength to live it more fully. Just accept that it will change you forever and that the change, while sometimes painful, will not necessarily be for the worse.

Accept That It Takes Time

When you burn your hand, you know it will take time to heal. In the same way, the recovery from emotional rape takes time. How much time depends on how badly you were burned.

You may be left with permanent scars, however that doesn't mean you can't live a fulfilled and happy life any more than having scars on your once-burned hand means you will not have the use and enjoyment of that hand. Those scars will serve as useful reminders to be more careful in the future.

The length of time taken to recover also depends on when the process of recovery begins. The recovery clock doesn't start the moment the hidden agenda is revealed; it begins when what happened is diagnosed as emotional rape.

Unfortunately, many victims endure years of pain in the aftermath of emotional rape without being correctly diagnosed, or having a single person understand what happened to them.

Seize the Moment—and Be Thankful

The only thing any of us has in this world is time, and we don't know exactly how much; it could be another forty-eight hours, could be another forty-eight years. However, we do know we don't want to waste whatever time we have struggling to cope with the aftermath of emotional rape.

We have to allow recovery all the time that is necessary, but not a minute more. Time is precious and, once lost, irretrievable. We should just be thankful we have time left in our lives—and seize the moment.

Dr. Bal Mount, one of the authors contributing to *Death—The Final Stage of Growth*, by Elisabeth Kubler-Ross, expresses this thought superbly. Diagnosed with a malignant tumor, Dr. Mount reasoned that the answer to the question, "How much time do I have?" is:

"There are 'x' days left, and however long 'x' is, there are only two possibilities, to live them in despair or to really live them to the hilt, making them count..."

Psychological Recovery 6

The Single Most Important Thing

Survivors of emotional rape face many mental and emotional challenges as they begin the process of recovery, and facing these challenges can result in positive personal growth, as discussed in the previous chapter.

First, however, they must acknowledge what really happened to them. There is no hope of recovery for someone who is suffering from cancer but being treated for influenza. We have to make a correct diagnosis before recovery can begin. The same holds true here.

If you are emotionally raped, the single most important thing to do is to accept that you are a rape victim and treat yourself accordingly.

This isn't always easy because our society finds it hard to accept that anyone is a totally innocent victim. It is popularly presumed that we all somehow contribute not only to our own problems, but to the problems of others as well, and there's some truth in this. But it isn't an argument that bears taking too far, as the following example demonstrates.

One spiritual advisor leading a church-sponsored

workshop on relationships and forgiveness lectured his audience on how there could be no such person as an "innocent victim." He maintained that the term is an oxymoron, a figure of speech combining apparently contradictory expressions. To be a victim is to be not innocent.

Many of those who attended the workshop had been shocked to hear, that morning at the Sunday service, about an eleven-year-old girl who was abducted from outside her home, and raped and murdered. However, when a member of the audience asked the workshop adviser if that girl was an innocent victim, he said she was not. Moreover, many in that audience obviously agreed with him that somehow she had been responsible for her fate. His argument was widely accepted.

The absurdity—indeed, the abhorrence—of that advisor's argument should surely be apparent. Sadly, there are people who take advantage of others, therefore there are victims.

The dangerous myth that we are all responsible for everything that happens to us has to be discredited conclusively, so victims—of emotional rape, for example—can learn to love and trust again, unencumbered by feelings of guilt and shame.

Believe You Didn't Do Anything Wrong

Remember that if you were emotionally raped you did not do anything morally wrong. Likewise, you are not foolish.

You gave honestly of yourself in a relationship, and your higher emotions, typically love and trust, were exploited. Giving of yourself is never foolish, nor something to be ashamed of; rather, it is generous and worthwhile.

If you believe in the existence of a Greater Power, perhaps the final judgment has still to be made about who truly profited or lost by the experience.

If you value highly your personal standards of goodness and fairness in dealing with others you may know already who won or lost in the relationship.

When someone commits an evil act against you, you are the victim, not the assailant nor co-assailant. Don't take seriously anyone who suggests otherwise. What they are saying will endanger rather than aid your eventual recovery.

Know What to Expect

Chapter Two discussed in detail what to expect in the aftermath of emotional rape. If you are a victim, re-read it often to remind yourself why you feel as you do, how your trauma is not unique to you, and that your pain will not last forever.

It is easy to become acutely depressed, even suicidal, if you believe the pain will never end, but remember that those victims who take their own lives chose a permanent solution to a temporary problem.

- Know what to expect.
- Know that your pain is not permanent and that you do have much to look forward to.
- Believe there is meaning and purpose to your life and that you can survive the darkest moments.
- Don't give up on yourself—recovery takes time.

Unlike sexual rape, it is difficult if not impossible to pinpoint the time and place where an emotional rape experience occurred. This trauma takes place over a much longer period and until now there may have been a blurring and confusing of what actually took place. The realization of what really happened may have been delayed.

This means the process of recovery may have been delayed as well and you may need to give yourself more time. However, have patience, and faith, and you will recover.

Recognize the Illusion of Control

Successful recovery requires acceptance of a number of paradoxes, the principal one being that to regain control of your life you have to accept your powerlessness in the face of the HALF factors (Health, Achievement, Love, and Faith).

It is this powerlessness that sets the stage for emotional rape.

We may have different degrees of power to resist each of the four HALF factors, but we should expect to be as powerless to resist at least one of them as any drug addict is to resist drugs.

This is an obvious analogy because most of what we know about powerlessness has been learned from individuals addicted to alcohol and other drugs. When drug addicts are actively using their substance of choice their minds are not their own; the addiction controls what they think, what they believe, and sometimes even what they perceive.

Recovered addicts understand what it means to be powerless.

Ironically, however, the substance seems to exercise power over the addict only for as long as he believes he is in control. So, for example, getting an alcoholic to see that he or she is not in control is an essential first step to abstinence from drink and thence recovery.

(One reason that drugs are such a major problem in many modern societies is that most people, addicts and non-addicts alike, believe an addict can resist the need for drugs. They believe in the illusion of control.)

Failing to see that we are powerless to resist the HALF factors is a barrier to recovery. It allows us to believe in the illusion of control and that is a foundation for depression.

Failure is inevitable when we cannot control something but believe we can.

Accepting our powerlessness eases the pain. Most alcoholics find it comforting to learn that they are suffering from a condition which makes them powerless to stop drinking; it means that they can stop blaming themselves and feeling weak, stupid, or destined to fail.

Similarly, emotional rape victims can stop feeling responsible for their trauma by recognizing that they were powerless to prevent what happened.

We Can Make Choices

Recognizing our powerlessness in the face of the HALF factors (Health, Achievement, Love, and Faith) is not to suggest we are addicted to them. They are simply essential to living, and are very often the basis for all that is beautiful and right in human existence: mutually supportive relationships, philanthropic actions, lifesaving medical discoveries, and so much more.

They are not substances like alcohol, or other drugs, that we can, or should, abstain from. Our need for them is more like an addiction to food, and if we totally abstain from food, we starve. If we abstain from love we starve emotionally, if we abstain from achievement we starve our self-esteem, abstinence from healthful living means becoming ill, and abstaining from faith risks our lives becoming meaningless.

A human being has to have HALF. However, just as we can make choices about the kinds of food we eat, we are able to make choices in other areas of our lives:

- We can choose the kind of people we allow into our lives, whom to love and from whom to accept love.
- We can decide the values we live by and make choices between good and evil.

It is only *after* we recognize that we are powerless, not before, that we become responsible for those choices.

Don't Accept Misuse of Our Needs

Identifying the HALF factors (Health, Achievement, Love, and Faith) and understanding that we may not have control over our need for them is just the beginning. It doesn't mean we have to accept everything that happens in the world.

- We are powerless in the face of our need for sex—but that doesn't mean we have to accept rape;
- We are powerless in the face of our need for food—but that doesn't mean we have to accept people dying of starvation;
- We are powerless in the face of our need for faith—but we don't have to accept the machinations of the Jimmy Swaggarts of this world;
- We are powerless in the face of our need for achievement—but we don't have to accept selfishness, dishonesty or manipulation in the desire for success.
- We are powerless in the face of our need for the HALF factors—but we don't have to accept emotional rape.

In other words, we don't have to accept the abuse of those things that we are powerless over. We don't have to accept evil.

Understand the Purpose of Pain: Damage Limitation

The purpose of physical pain is obvious: it tells you that something is not right in your physical world. When you put your hand on a hot stove, the pain makes you move it—fast—before it is badly burned. If there were no pain to warn you, it would be the smell of charred flesh that told you, too late, that you were causing yourself lasting injury.

Just as physical pain has a purpose, so does emotional pain. It warns you that something is not right in your emotional world. If the realization that you were emotionally raped wasn't painful the rape might continue, allowing the rapist to plunder even greater expanses of your life.

Pain limits damage, both emotional and physical.

However, just as a burned hand hurts for a while afterwards, so do burned emotions. Healing takes time, but the pain you experience is valuable to your survival.

If you burn your hand on a stove, you're going to think twice about putting it down on another stove, which is good. If you are burned emotionally, you are going to be careful what you do with your emotions for a while. That isn't bad either.

It is when the ability to feel pain is impaired that the consequences can be serious.

There are many things that can dull our physical warning system, including illness, disability, fatigue and intoxication. If you were intoxicated, for example, when you put your hand on that hot stove, you might leave it there for longer than you would if you were sober. You might get more seriously burned.

Similarly, if your emotional warning system becomes dulled, you are more likely to be badly hurt emotionally...

Understand What Dulls Your Emotional Warning System

We are surrounded by individual and social values that dull our emotional warning system. They are everywhere, so prevalent that we often have difficulty seeing them, even those which do not serve us well.

In this age of mass communication we are bombarded with messages exalting very questionable values; messages seeking to attract, manipulate and dishonestly persuade us to respond in a particular way.

Significantly, this is also the *modus operandi* of the

emotional rapist, and, because attraction, manipulation and dishonesty are everywhere, he or she is not likely to be easily identified. On the contrary, a rapist might even be admired in some quarters, rather than held in universal contempt, if he or she is exposed.

For example, a woman who used love for financial gain, who married for money, might be considered shrewd and successful rather than deceitful and calculating. (Indeed, a popular television talk show promoted such behavior—more of which is in Chapter Eleven, which focuses on society's value system and how it can facilitate, even sanction, emotional rape.)

Cheryl's story highlights the connection between emotional rape and personal/social values.

She revealed that before she met Robert she made a list of all the things she looked for in her ideal man. Robert seemed to possess all those attributes. However, Cheryl admitted later: "The only thing I didn't have on my list was values."

The result, as we saw in Chapter Two, was disastrous. Cheryl got involved with a superficially attractive, materialistic person who discarded her as soon as he met someone who offered him more.

Communicate

Sharing your feelings can accelerate the recovery process, but it is important to choose your confidants carefully.

Not everyone will understand what has happened to you and those who don't might withdraw when you reveal how you really feel. Certainly, pouring out your innermost feelings indiscriminately will only scare many people away, probably leaving you even more isolated and hurt.

Someone who has gone through a similar experience may be your best choice, if you know such a person well enough. Going to a professional counselor might be a good investment if you don't have such a friend.

Whomever you choose, don't be afraid to ask for help. Just telling someone you are hurting and need to talk can bring great relief.

Writing can also be useful therapy. Many people who have suffered in life have found recording their experiences on paper contributed a great deal to their recovery. The actress Theresa Saldana wrote *Beyond Survival* during her recovery from a vicious knife attack, and singer Barbara Mandrel published a book about her recovery from a crippling automobile accident.

Keeping a daily journal helps to keep track of your recovery and forces you to clarify your feelings to put them into words, a process which in turn helps you communicate more effectively with others.

Go Ahead, Get Mad

Anger is a powerful force and not necessarily a destructive one. It can be a fantastic source of energy for positive change. Denying your anger only prolongs the recovery process and can cause depression. Find a way to use its power positively and turn it into achievement:

- Start a program of regular exercise.
- Write that book you've been planning for years.
- Learn to play a musical instrument.
- Help others to recover from emotional rape.
- Go ahead, get mad. Let your anger propel you in new directions.

Historically, much of the man-made beauty in the world was born out of pain. Many great artists and writers were driven by their emotional torment. Your pain and anger presents an opportunity to tap into a great resource of emotional energy and inspiration that is not available to you on an everyday basis.

Think 'Willingness'

If all this sounds like good theory, but you can't see any obvious practical way to harness your emotional energy, try the immediate release of exercise.

Go for a good walk, and while you're walking be willing to direct your anger and pain into something constructive. Repeat a simple statement of purpose, like: "I must channel all this into something good. I mustn't let it go to waste."

Before long, if you are willing to use your anger and pain to positive purpose, you won't have to guess which way to go. Just be willing to move on and the right direction will become clear.

Remember your anger and pain won't last forever, so you must take advantage of this energy while you can. And don't let the misdirected blame of others, or your own tendency towards self-blame, turn that anger inward against yourself.

Harold Kushner perfectly expresses this positive mind set in *Why Bad Things Happen To Good People*. Whenever time is short but you need motivation try rereading the following excerpt—a marvelously succinct expression of the value of channeling bad into good:

The bad things that happen to us in our lives do not have a meaning when they happen to us...But we can give them a meaning. We can redeem these tragedies from senselessness by imposing meaning on them.

The question we should be asking is not "Why did this happen to me? What did I do to deserve this?" That is really an unanswerable, pointless question. A better question would be "Now that this has happened to me, what am I going to do about it?"

Acknowledge Your Fears

In the aftermath of emotional rape, fear and anxiety may engulf you, and the fact that those around you may not understand, or be willing to accept, your fears can exacerbate the situation.

However, if we deny our fears, we are ruled by them. Rather, we have to acknowledge that we are afraid, then our fears can be transformed; initially into anger, then to positive actions.

The only negative emotions are those that remain unexpressed, or *un-transformed.* The ideal way to express them is to transform them into a positive force.

Feeling afraid and anxious at times is just part of being human; acknowledge your humanity and put it to good use.

The Inability to Love or Trust: Accept the Loss is Temporary

If you were emotionally raped, you desperately want and need to trust someone—anyone. However, because another person abused your trust and love you will be reluctant to develop these feelings towards anyone else. Acknowledge this reluctance, don't deny it, lest feelings are neglected and surface unexpectedly in the future, possibly with disastrous consequences.

Losing the ability to love or trust is probably the greatest loss in emotional rape. Certainly, it is a major factor in cases where victims are eventually driven to attempt suicide.

When this ability is damaged we feel it immediately, and we are suddenly unable to generate love in our lives, but almost all survivors have experienced this loss, and in almost all cases it was temporary. It has to be expected and accepted.

Restoring Order Amid Confusion

Confusion, like struggle and adversity, is not necessarily bad. Indeed, it is when we are the most confused that we are the most open to enlightenment and positive change.

If nothing else, emotional rape forces survivors to re-examine their values, the purpose of their lives, and their goals; having your life shaken up provides a rare opportunity to decide where you want the pieces to fall.

Many survivors say they learned a lot about themselves in the traumatic aftermath and some admit they found their old values to be shallow and inadequate.

Some changed their profession, others changed where they lived. As might be expected, most changed the priorities they used to decide which people they let into their lives. One said: "I feel as if my whole life, even who I am, is being changed before my very eyes."

Think of the confusion that you are experiencing as part of the transformation of who you are.

Like the butterfly emerging from the cocoon, you may feel uncertain about this metamorphosis at first, but the potential for beauty and wonderful flight is there. All it needs is acceptance and appropriate action for new strength, new direction, and new achievements to emerge with the new you.

Don't worry about the day-to-day confusion, the little things like missed exits on the freeway, misplaced purses and spectacles, forgotten appointments. Just be aware of such possibilities and guard against them:

- Make checklists. Tape one to your front door, perhaps, reminding you to make sure all the lights are out, that the stove is turned off, and that the doors and windows are locked before you go out.
- Check to be sure you have your keys to get back in.
- Hide an extra set of door keys outside your home and tape an extra set of car keys to the underside of your car.

- When you can't write things down (for example, when you are driving), pocket-size cassette tape recorders are useful to record your thoughts and list the tasks you have to do.
- If you need to remind yourself about jobs to do when you get home, leave messages on your own answering machine.

Have faith that the everyday incidents of confusion will become less and less frequent as you channel your emotional energy in positive directions.

Turn Losses into Opportunities

The losses suffered by victims of emotional rape can be tangible as well as intangible.

Intangible losses, like losing the ability to love and trust, may make you feel you'll never be able to give of yourself the way you once did.

The tangible losses, like money, property and time, are traumatic enough in normal circumstances; they can be particularly stressful for the individual struggling to cope as well with the aftermath of emotional rape. Feelings of confusion and depression are understandable.

However, material losses can be regained in some cases, particularly when the power of anger is being channeled towards new achievements. For example, you might make up financial losses by channeling more energy into advancing your career.

Loss makes room for creation: new jobs, new relationships, new challenges and experiences. You can replace those losses and bring those qualities back into your life— in time.

Starting to Love and Trust Again

The realization that someone you loved and trusted could so deliberately wreck your life intensifies the sense of loss and betrayal.

Nevertheless, your damaged emotions will be repaired, and restored even stronger than they were before, because you generate love from within. While you may have temporarily lost your willingness to generate love, you have not lost your ability to do so.

We cannot give that ability away, nor can it be taken by others—it can only be denied to us by ourselves. Because you were once capable of generating the love that your rapist used against you, you will be capable of generating love again. Think of it as having been "frozen"—preserved until you are ready to use it again.

- Just believe in yourself and allow yourself time. You can't deny that a great void has been created in your emotional world and you may feel unworthy of love, or fear what others think about you. However, trust that this void will be filled as you recover and are transformed.

- There is no need to fear new relationships, but don't try to force them. Simply be willing to have them and let them happen when the time feels right. Go slowly, be prudent, and be aware. Check your values. Study Chapter Fourteen for advice on self-defense.

- Do the things that you enjoy doing. Not only will you have a better chance of meeting someone you are compatible with, but you will be an altogether happier person to be with.

- Tell yourself that if you give up, the evil ones have won. Keep believing in your ability to love, to survive the rapist's exploitation—even to thrive upon it—and to find new and better ways to create love in your life.

Don't Fight Loneliness

Recognizing our powerlessness in the face of the HALF factors (Health, Achievement, Love, and Faith) results in a new sense of freedom and peace. After all, why should we accept responsibility for filling needs that we didn't create in the first place? Why should we have to feel like failures, for example, because we don't have a romantic relationship?

We can let go, learn to live with our needs, and learn how to be alone. Loneliness is not a condition to be avoided at all costs—accept it. Being alone is an opportunity to experience yourself, to experience your own wholeness.

Paradoxically, the ability to be truly alone with oneself is a precondition for the ability to love. As noted by Erich Fromm, if we are incapable of being alone and standing on our own two feet, we will build relationships on need rather than love.

Victims of emotional rape typically need some time to be alone, even lonely, to resolve their confusion and begin to heal their own wounds. This loneliness will not last long if we accept it as part of the emotional pain needed for growth, then channel it in positive directions.

Socialize From Strength

All this is not to suggest you have to become a hermit. It's another paradox that we often enjoy the greatest success in a particular area of our lives when we feel comfortable and relaxed.

Once you accept that you are comfortable with or without a relationship, you will become more relaxed in the company of other people.

The more relaxed and comfortable you become, the more other people will want to be around you, and the more opportunities there will be for friendships and social relationships.

Consider the butterfly that you just can't catch, but which just *might* land on your shoulder if you sit still long enough. Commonsense should tell you, however, that if you want a butterfly to land on your shoulder, eventually you have to be where the butterflies are.

- Concentrate on renewing old friendships.

- Call those friends you have been meaning to contact for ages, but haven't. Meet for lunch, or get together for a sports event or movie.

- Catch up with your family. If you can't visit in person, be sure to call. Taking an interest in their lives can take much of the stress out of yours.

- Recognize that your exercise program can be an opportunity for social contact. Tennis, golf, body building, aerobics, biking, hiking, and walking are all sports for which you can generally find clubs or classes.

- Finally, if you like animals, your recovery period could be a great time to adopt a pet; one which is just enough of a loving nuisance to keep you from getting too lonely. There are plenty of abandoned dogs and cats at the Humane Society that would agree.

Laugh: it is the Best Medicine

It is difficult to see the humor in emotional rape, but you can find it. Fortunately, there is humor in almost everything, and targets are everywhere: attorneys, the legal system, the other man, the other woman, psychologists and counselors, society, the government... emotional rapists. And, of course, ourselves. In many cases victims meet others who have been through the same trauma and, in sharing their common experience, find themselves discovering inherent humor in their situations.

If you plan to see a movie with friends or family, pick a comedy. Video your comedy favorites when they appear on television and watch them at your leisure.

Laughter really is good medicine. Keeping a sense of humor can help keep you sane.

Pamper Yourself

If you were recovering from a severe physical illness your doctor would want you to eat healthy, nutritious foods. In the same way, if you are recovering from emotional rape, you need to feed yourself positive mental food.

You have already been through a lot of pain and more than any other time in your life you have the right to pamper yourself:

- Instead of listening to rock and pop songs—most of which tell us we're nothing without someone or something to love—on the radio, try something new, like recordings of classical or instrumental music, or songs with positive messages.

  When you're driving, choose positive music for your car cassette or compact disc player.

- Invest in a tape-alarm clock so you wake up in the morning to some inspiring music.

  One survivor woke up either to the theme from the *Rocky* movies or to the classic ballad *What a Wonderful World*, sung by Louis Armstrong; music that made her feel positive and motivated. If you are the type who involuntarily has songs going through your mind all day, they might as well have a positive effect.

- Consider using a meditation and self-hypnosis tape.

  Another survivor reported a marked improvement in his mood and mental attitude after he played the tape when he went to bed. As well as giving him positive messages, it helped him fall asleep. There are subliminal self-hypnosis tapes available in versions that are safe to listen to while driving.

■ Treat yourself to a reasonably priced present; some new clothes can be a good investment.

■ If possible, take a vacation. Look into packaged vacations that take care of all the detailed arrangements so you will be as free of stress as possible.

■ Take yourself and a friend out to brunch, or go to a matinee movie during the week.

■ Redecorate your home. A new look sometimes helps to clean out painful memories. Little things, like new wall hangings, can make a big difference.

■ Educate yourself. Take a class in something that you've always wanted to learn. Expose yourself to excellence and creativity through symphonies, musicals, plays, fine art and athletic events.

A warning, though: don't let these treats and new experiences strain your budget. Inexpensive items and events can make you feel just as good as big, expensive ones, and the last thing you need is the extra worry of being in debt.

Take it Easy

Occasionally, you'll have a particularly difficult day, and being generous to yourself means not worrying about admitting defeat and cutting short the rest of your plans.

Acknowledge that a bad day is not going to be a productive one—then take it easy.

Focus on the future by making a list of things to do tomorrow. Decide your priorities so you'll be sure to do the most important things first, just in case you run out of energy again.

Occasionally, make a point of going to bed earlier than usual and reading something positive. Straighten up the house so you don't have much to do first thing in the morning. Select the clothes you plan to wear the next day. Having everything clean and ready to greet you in the morning is a pleasant start to any day.

Revenge

Forget it. Preoccupying yourself with thoughts of revenge is an understandable, but non-constructive, response to your suffering; one that only prolongs the recovery process. Let it go. Stop saying "If only"—start saying "Next time."

If your actions in the past were generous and kind, dwelling on thoughts of retribution and inflicting pain compromises your own goodness and you sink towards the moral level of the rapist.

Don't give in to evil, that would only cancel all the credit you have built up in your spiritual savings account.

Release

Revenge should not be confused with release. Although release doesn't necessarily transform anger into anything positive for the survivor, it can occasionally be therapeutic to dissipate pent-up feelings of anger and rage.

For example, one woman who grew up on a farm and was used to handling guns took a photograph of her emotional rapist to the shooting range. "My very first shot was right on target...and it felt damn good," she said.

Shooting pictures, and other forms of emotional release, is certainly preferable to bottling up powerful feelings. But, as we saw earlier, it is much better to find a constructive outlet for this tremendous gift of energy.

Cry If You Want To

Another form of release is crying. If you can, do it.

Even when you are alone, letting it all out through tears can be therapeutic, perhaps essential.

Forgiveness

The person you most need to forgive is yourself and once you do this you will be ready to go on with your life and grow.

- Forgive yourself for not seeing the truth; accept that you were powerless.
- Forgive yourself for being angry and human.

In the unlikely event that the individual who raped you sincerely asks for your forgiveness, of course give it, if you so wish. However, it is not required of you to unilaterally forgive anyone unless you choose to do so.

At some point you will be able to accept that your rapist was a sick person, unable to love himself (or herself) and therefore incapable of loving others. You will regard that person as a lonely individual who can never have a truly worthwhile relationship and who is afraid to be who he (or she) really is.

When that happens you will have, unintentionally, forgiven your rapist.

Just Do It

What does it mean to be willing to recover from emotional rape?

Willingness is a desire of sufficient intensity to be translated into action.

This doesn't mean taking things to extremes: quitting

a secure job to try to become the world's leading entrepreneur, or going out every night searching for the most loving relationship in history.

It means doing those things that are obvious and that you have no excuse not to do:

■ Like... exercise.

■ Like... eating right.

■ Like... being sure you expose yourself only to low-key social situations.

■ Like... not drinking to excess, and not taking drugs.

■ Like... being nice to yourself.

Tackling even the most mundane activity can be beneficial.

Cleaning out a closet may not seem like much, but it is better than doing nothing, and when you've completed the job you will have a modest sense of accomplishment. Moving forward just an inch at a time is still progress, and you can move a considerable distance in one-inch "steps."

One survivor told how he became very depressed. Because he had plenty of time (he had been disabled from his job) he decided to rebuild an old fence. The work got him out of the house and digging the new holes gave him some much-needed exercise. He got tanned, lost a few pounds, and when he finished the job he felt a sense of achievement that raised his sense of self-esteem.

Of course, fence repair did not solve all his problems, but it was a step in the right direction; and he did finish up with a great-looking fence. He later described the project as a definite turning point in his emotional recovery.

He had done *something*—he had taken action.

Physical Recovery 7

The Stress Threat

Emotional rape is a very serious business. If you are its victim, what has happened is undoubtedly putting extreme stress on you at this moment—and stress kills. Stress has been linked to disease and death, and, no matter what happened to you, it isn't worth the sacrifice of your life or your health.

Starting right now, you must begin to take care of yourself physically, as well as emotionally.

This is perhaps the most practical chapter of our guide, examining the vital importance to recovery of taking care of your physical well-being.

Exercise

If you are under stress and haven't been getting enough exercise, your wisest move would be to put down this book and start a new fitness regime straightaway. If you can't do it this second, make a solemn promise to begin first thing in the morning.

Make exercise an enjoyable part of your lifestyle, always remembering:

- If you have doubts about performing any type of exercise consult your physician first.
- Never exercise against the advice of a physician.
- Stop if you feel any sort of pain or discomfort while exercising.

Exercise is a great stress-reliever. It not only has measurable physical benefits, but it is also emotionally therapeutic. It can help you achieve your optimum weight and get into shape. You'll look and feel better, which helps to rebuild any damaged sense of self-esteem.

If there is no other form of exercise that you prefer, start by walking on a daily basis.

Go out for about twenty minutes to begin with, walking at a brisk pace to raise your pulse rate. Every other day, walk for a bit longer, even if the increase is only a fraction of a minute, and you'll soon be able to walk comfortably for an hour a day. Maintain that level.

If you have any joint problems, with your knees, for example, try swimming.

Swimming is a great exercise for the cardiovascular system and the gentle buoyancy of the water supports your body, taking much of the strain off your joints. There's none of the bone-jarring impact involved in pounding the sidewalks on a running or jogging session.

If you have easy access to a pool, you might want to start a regular swimming program, or try a combination of swimming and walking on alternate days. Variety helps to keep regular exercising fun.

Aerobics is also beneficial. The combination of upbeat music and exercise is definitely therapeutic, both physically and emotionally, and classes also get you out among other people.

(Keep in mind that many forms of exercise provide safe

social interaction. For example, going for regular work-outs at a health club, attending dance classes or joining the local tennis club will almost certainly involve a so-cial, as well as physical, element.)

Don't overestimate your abilities and enroll in an ad-vanced aerobics class, or any other advanced exercise class, if you know you are out of condition. Start in the be-ginners' class and move up, if you want to, as your level of fitness improves.

It's important to avoid injuring or straining yourself, whether you're exercising on aerobics mats, out walking, or in the pool.

Getting injured means having to give up your regular exercise until the injury heals, which only adds feelings of frustration and disappointment to your other problems.

The Choice is Yours

It's neither necessary nor possible to list all the exercise options available to you. There are dozens of books and magazines devoted to particular activities, and thousands of well-organized health clubs and spas all over the coun-try, where qualified exercise instructors can draw up a program to match your needs.

With a little dedication, you're sure to find an activity that works for you. The difficult part is getting started and developing the self-discipline to stick to your program of exercise as planned, whether those plans call for daily sessions, every-other-day sessions, or whatever.

Always remember that exercising regularly is much more important than working out so hard that it becomes a chore.

Start slowly. If you are consistent, you'll find yourself gradually doing more and more in natural, painless in-crements. This isn't Olympic training—you are just trying to get your life back together.

Diet

Eating a nutritionally balanced diet can help counteract the damaging effects of stress, and, at the risk of laboring the point, stress can seriously affect your physical health.

In their book *Is It Worth Dying For?* Dr. Robert Eliot and Dennis Breo point out that short and long term stress has been shown to increase adrenaline and cortisol levels in the body.

Adrenaline increases the stickiness of blood-clotting fragments and cortisol can increase their number; the net result being that you drastically increase your chance of heart-related illness.

Once again there is a multitude of publications—books, magazines and newsletters—which give good advice about what, and how much, we should eat for optimum health. There are also many experts—dietitians and doctors, to name but two—who can dispense their valuable advice face-to-face, specifically for you.

The following are general guidelines:

■ First, our concern is not with any kind of crash diet plan, such as those heavily advertised on television. The main thing is to think about your health when you are making decisions about what to eat.

■ Avoid those foods that are not good for your heart; that is, foods containing high levels of fat.

■ Eat less sugar and sweets.

■ Eat more fruits and vegetables.

■ Eat more grains and cereals.

■ Try to eat more fish and poultry and less red meat and fried food.

■ Avoid foods like ice cream and cut back on other dairy products like milk, cheese and sour cream.

■ Avoid chocolate.

But these are all your favorites, right? Fortunately,

you don't have to feel too deprived because simple substitutions can do wonders to satisfy the taste buds:

- Choose non-fat yogurt instead of ice cream, for example, or low-fat spread instead of full cream butter.
- Consider also taking a daily multivitamin tablet, some vitamin E, and a vitamin B stress complex.
- Don't overdo it with large doses, just take what you need to make up any possible deficiencies in your diet.

Establish a Routine

When you are under mental and emotional stress establishing regular routines can be helpful.

For example, go to bed at about the same time every night, preferably early. Prepare your clothes, lunch, and meet-ing notes the night before. Get up at a regular hour and follow a set morning routine.

Before you leave work, plan your timetable for the following day, and, if possible, schedule your most exacting work tasks early in the day.

A regular lunch time walk might be beneficial, clearing your head and calming you down for the afternoon's endeavors.

Plan your exercise sessions for the same time every day and allow time for relaxing meditation.

Avoid Dependency...

The aftermath of emotional rape may be a particularly difficult time to give up certain pleasures. Conversely, it could be the best opportunity to do just that.

Remember, any relief you experience from addictive substances is only temporary, then your body demands more. Such substances can also cloud your judgment at a time when, more than ever, you need to be able to think clearly. Avoid dependency...

...on Drugs and Alcohol

If you feel you might have a problem with drugs or alcohol, dial directory assistance and ask for the local number of Alcoholics Anonymous or Rational Recovery. Within minutes you can be talking to somebody who will truly appreciate what you are going through because he or she has been in exactly the same situation.

Although AA used to be concerned only with alcoholic abuse, many people today are dual-addicted to both alcohol and drugs. If for some reason AA can't help, someone in that organization will be able to tell you who can. Don't be afraid to ask.

Having a problem with drugs or alcohol does not make you a weak person. You just happen to be powerless over a substance, in very much the same way we are all powerless in the face of the HALF factors (Health, Achievement, Love, and Faith).

But do seek help. Getting used by a substance isn't any less harmful than getting used by another person.

...on Caffeine

If you're congratulating yourself on not being addicted to drugs or alcohol, that's great.

However, you may be less pleased to learn that caffeine, which is actually a poison, produces a stimulating effect similar to some drugs. When dosed on coffee, the body releases adrenaline to help combat the caffeine.

An excess of caffeine also contributes to your levels of anxiety; in other words, if you are already under stress, adding too much caffeine to your system could make things worse.

If you find it impossible to give up caffeine altogether, try to reduce your intake. Many coffee drinkers have found that a 50/50 blend of regular/decaffeinated coffee satisfies their addiction while considerably reducing their caffeine intake. It gets you going without the jangles. You can even ask your waitress for a cup of 50/50 when eating out; it's becoming commonplace.

Also be aware that coffee has other chemicals in it besides caffeine and some of them also affect the heart—more good reasons to reduce your overall intake of coffee, even the 50/50 blend. Tea, chocolate and some soft drinks also contain caffeine.

...on Nicotine

Nicotine, in tobacco, is one of the most addictive substances known to man, said to be even more addictive than heroin. Indeed, it's amazing that tobacco is legal; nicotine is nothing but bad for you, constricting the blood vessels and capillaries.

Some survivors of emotional rape recall their smoking increased during the aftermath, so, if you are a smoker, you may find it difficult even to cut down, let alone stop. However, keep in mind that these are very stressful times for your heart and circulatory system, and your body needs all the help it can get.

...on Food

Don't binge. Survivors also report that they began eating much more and many say they developed a particular craving for sweet, sugary foods.

These binges usually occur later, some time after the initial shock, and can result in considerable weight gains that have a negative effect on self-esteem, possibly leading to further eating sprees. A depressing spiral.

Emotional rape makes victims typically feel angry, vulnerable and depressed, but seeking any sort of solace through excessive use of alcohol, drugs or food, is counterproductive.

Prescription Drugs

Control your dependence on prescription drugs as much as possible. Some doctors are more than willing to prescribe mood-altering drugs, which you may, or may not, need.

Use common sense:

Before you start using tranquilizers, reduce your intake of coffee and other sources of caffeine to see if that has any useful effect.

Before you begin taking antidepressants, be sure you are not depressing yourself chemically with alcohol or street drugs, and that you are getting sufficient exercise.

If you are depressed or excessively anxious even though you have been exercising regularly, avoiding alcohol and street drugs, and not using caffeine, consult your doctor. You may indeed need the help of a prescription for a short time, until your life becomes less stressful.

Before starting any prescription, find out about any known side effects.

This is important. If you experience obvious mood changes and do not know what is causing them you may decide to increase your dose, which will only make the situation worse. (It is never advisable, under any circumstances, to change the dosage of a prescription drug without consulting your doctor.)

Ask your doctor, or ask the pharmacist for a data sheet on that particular drug when you get the prescription filled. These sheets are available for all prescription medicines and describe how a drug works and its potential side effects.

When you are already struggling with strong feelings of anger and anxiety, antidepressants are not always the best answer. They can make some people short-tempered, tense and impatient. Heart palpitations can also occur. On very rare occasions one prescribed antidepressant, Prozac, has caused patients to suffer suicidal tendencies.

Relax—Take a Break

Make time to relax. If you have accrued vacation time at work, now is a good time to use it. Take a trip to a sun resort, a cruise, or a similar break.

If you can, talk to your employer about what you are going through. It's not necessary to be specific, just explain that you are under stress and offer as many reasons as you feel comfortable sharing. How much you share will inevitably depend on your relationship with your immediate boss and with your employer.

If relations between you are at all adversarial it is advisable to visit your doctor and get a proper medical prescription for some time off before approaching your employer.

Don't jeopardize your job.

It's an unfortunate fact that there are employers who will lay off an employee when they find out he or she may have to take time off due to medical disability, or has a problem that may cause a drop in his or her personal productivity.

If you have accrued sick days ask your doctor to prescribe some time off work. Almost any doctor will do this without hesitation if you explain the situation. An understanding employer might let you take your accrued sick time without seeing your doctor, but it is best to err on the side of caution and obtain a prescription first, if only to ensure your rights to benefits are protected.

Only you can determine the best course of action, based upon your relationship with your employer and on your employer's reputation for having reacted sympathetically, or otherwise, in previous similar cases.

Medical Leave

If you feel you are about to lose control of your situation, that things are really getting on top of you, ask your doctor about taking a longer break from work.

One victim went on long-term medical leave after struggling for almost a year with the aftermath of emotional rape. She finally realized she was in such a terrible mental state that she was doing more damage to her career by continuing to work than by taking a long time off.

She was fortunate enough to have a sympathetic employer and was able to take one year off, on sixty percent pay, through the company's disability insurance program—time which proved instrumental in her recovery.

She now believes that period of leave was the best thing she ever did, for her career as well as her emotional well-being.

Get Some Sun

In his book *Light—Medicine of the Future*, Dr. Jacob Liberman points out that modern-day living has taken us out of the natural sunlight and put us under artificial light, creating a condition he identifies as "malillumination" or "sunlight starvation."

Natural sunlight, he maintains, is essential for our physical and mental well-being; for survivors of emotional rape it can be particularly therapeutic.

If the climate allows, make a point of getting outside into the sun at least every other day. Not only does it feel good, it also forces you to relax and gives you a healthy-looking, light tan which helps you look and feel better.

The emphasis here is on sensible, short exposure in moderate sun—not lying out in a swimsuit for hours in 100° temperatures. Like everything else, the sun can be extremely harmful if it is indulged in to excess.

The basic advice is always to protect yourself by applying a sunscreen of suitable strength for your skin type, and, at least to start with, only to stay out in the sun for a very short time. Avoid exposure in the hours just before and after noon, when the sun is at its highest and the danger of burning is greatest.

If you live in a cool climate, dark overcast days can definitely make it more difficult to get over feelings of depression and anxiety. Apart from reading Dr. Liberman's book (it's an excellent aid to understanding the role of light in health), consider replacing the lights in your home and office with full-spectrum light sources and, as suggested above, try to get away for a vacation in a sunnier climate.

Listen to Your Body

Looking after yourself can brighten the emotional darkness in the aftermath of any emotional or physical trauma—just as sunlight brightens our days.

Paying attention to your physical well-being also helps you feel better psychologically.

Believe that you deserve some special treatment:

- Exercise regularly
- Eat a nutritionally balanced diet.
- Establish a regular daily routine.
- Avoid dependency on drugs, alcohol, caffeine, nicotine and food, especially foods containing a lot of sugar.
- Use prescription drugs wisely, and under a doctor's supervision.
- Try to relax; take a break in the sun.

Above all, listen to your body and keep it healthy.

Recovery:
Outside Help 8

Why Look to Others?

This chapter looks at some of the outside agencies and individuals that survivors might turn to for help with the process of recovery, and points out some of the perils and pitfalls of enlisting outside help.

The reactions of others can sometimes seem negative and critical, perhaps even depressing and it is as well to prepare for such a possibility. As always, it pays to expect the unexpected.

The aftermath of emotional rape, as we have seen, is a serious situation. Surviving it alone can be very difficult.

If we have influenza, our body's amazing ability to heal itself usually handles the recovery process and we get better on our own with a few days rest. However, for more serious conditions we need help from a medical specialist. We can't recover alone, and we are unlikely to get help if we don't actively seek it.

If possible, the first step is to find a friend you can talk to, someone who will listen without making judgments about you or the situation, someone you can trust to be supportive; a friend who can help you restore your life.

Prepare for the Unexpected

Be forewarned, however, that even the truest of friends may not be able to accept you are a victim.

For others, accepting that you were emotionally raped means acknowledging that, someday, they might also face the same traumatic situation—that it could happen to them, or even that they could become a rapist themselves. Most people would prefer to avoid such uncomfortable admissions.

You are not to blame if they can't accept that what happened to you was a form of rape. You don't have to change your position because they don't agree with you, and neither should you blame them for their beliefs. They are not at fault any more than you are, they have simply reacted in an understandable and predictable way.

Typical responses might include: "Just put it behind you... There are plenty more fish in the sea... Just pull yourself up by your boot straps... It takes two to tango... What is it about you that is attracted to a person like that?... Maybe God is trying to teach you a lesson... He doesn't give anything to anyone that they can't handle."

Remember that your friends really are trying to help, although their observations will probably only make you feel responsible or weak.

Take comfort in knowing that they care about you, even if they don't fully understand the trauma you are going through. They don't realize that much of what they say may only make things worse, so you have to be bigger than they are.

They have reasons for saying these things. They may find it easier to blame you than to accept other alternatives. After all, if you didn't deserve what happened to you, they must be living in a random and meaningless world. Or perhaps they believe that God is all powerful, in control of everything, and does not let anything happen to anyone without good reason.

They cannot blame God, so they have to blame you and you will have to listen to quasi-philosophical arguments—word games—the purpose of which will surely be to "prove" that, far from being evil, what happened to you was part of His grand design (even though no one will be able to explain exactly what that design involves).

These theories deny the existence of evil and inevitably lead to apportioning blame to the victim.

As the following case illustrates, there is a powerful need *not* to believe in the reality of emotional rape.

Anita and Mark: the Desire NOT to Know

Anita and Mark had been married for five years and, like many couples, had problems which prompted them to seek counseling.

However, after they completed a one-week retreat where they renewed their marriage vows and had their union blessed by a priest, Anita thought she had every reason to be optimistic about the future—until she made a shocking discovery.

While Mark was away on business, she found a copy of a wedding invitation: it was *his* wedding, to another woman, Iris, and the big day was just two weeks away.

Anita later recalled feeling as if she had been hit in the stomach with a club, the discovery was so painful to her.

Moreover, it emerged that this was far from being the full extent of Mark's deception. In fact he had had two marriages to two different women scheduled for that same day, but had already sent a note to the second bride-to-be, Rose, saying he couldn't go through with their wedding.

However, Rose knew about Anita (Mark had told her he and Anita had divorced) and about one of his ex-girl-friends, Jane (whom he had secretly continued to date). Thinking they might have some idea what caused Mark to change his mind, Rose called both of them and when the three women got together and compared notes it became clear they had all been deceived.

Rose and Jane helped Anita pack Mark's bags. They all saw themselves as "Mark victims," and agreed they would support each other in their attempts to recover from their experiences.

They also agreed to write to Iris, who was not aware of Mark's wholesale deception and still planned to marry him. In their letter they told her everything they knew about Mark and offered her their support, but there was no response.

Eventually, Rose telephoned and was stunned by the reaction. Iris explained: "Look, I'm thirty-eight years old and I have never been married. This is it." She married Mark just two days after his divorce from Anita was final.

Denial in All its Glory

Iris's attitude was denial in all its glory: an intense desire *not* to know resulting from her powerlessness to resist one of the HALF factors (Health, Achievement, Love, and Faith)—in this case love—and from a sadly distorted scale of values.

On the face of it, her behavior was incomprehensible. How could she possibly believe that being married was more important than the moral integrity—the amoral capability, in Mark's case—of the man she was about to marry?

However, Mark offers one more example of the deceiver as charismatic charmer. All his victims described him as good-looking and intelligent, outwardly gentle and cultured. And Iris, of all four women, had the most to lose, so she did not want to face the painful truth that the man she loved might not love her. She was a person in the process of being victimized herself yet would not accept the reality of her situation, despite the overwhelming evidence of three independent testimonies.

As a victim, don't be surprised if your friends and family have a similar capacity for ignoring the reality of emotional rape. It would be unreasonable to expect them to be any less blind in the face of the truth than was Iris—or any less blind than you were when the act of rape was taking place. (This is particularly true if they might have an uncomfortable feeling that they themselves are in a potentially harmful relationship.)

Don't use up valuable energy encouraging such people to see the light; you have enough to cope with already. Instead, you might suggest they read this book to get a better understanding of what has happened to you and what you are going through.

In any event, just accept that friends and family care about you, which in itself is cause for genuine celebration. And never forget: you don't have to abandon the belief that you have been emotionally raped just because others don't agree with you.

Professional Counseling

There are times in our lives when we need a trained observer to help us to see what we can't see for ourselves, or to show us where we are making things more difficult than they need to be.

This is the specific area of expertise of the professional therapist, psychiatrist, or psychologist, and to make sure the professional you turn to is right for you, consider the following:

Your counselor should be licensed and registered with the State.

This may prove important if you need to take time off work or go on long-term medical leave. It's a good idea to get into therapy early in the recovery process to protect your long-term medical benefits in case you need them at some point in the future.

Counseling for emotional rape is in its infancy.

If psychologists and psychiatrists have a well-developed program of recovery for emotional rape, it is a well-kept secret. There are many good counselors but it can be hard to find the right one.

Look for counselors who provide therapy for sexual rape victims.

Avoid counselors whose preferred methodology is to focus on what is wrong with the victim.

At some stage you will need to examine your own role in the rape experience, but beginning your therapy with that emphasis will surely make things worse.

What is needed is a program to aid recovery, not a program to establish blame.

Make it clear to your therapist from the outset that you consider yourself to be a victim of emotional rape and that you want to be treated like a rape victim.

Try to find a counselor who uses a peer support group approach.

Talking and sharing your feelings with others who have had the same experience works wonders.

Trust Your Instincts

When you're a hammer, everything looks like a nail.

Or, in other words, the world can look very different according to your point of view. So bear in mind that the treatment provided for almost any ailment, physical or emotional, will depend on the attitudes and professional preferences of the particular healer.

A nutritionist will prescribe nutrition. A psycho-pharmacologist will prescribe drugs. A priest will prescribe prayer. A massage therapist will prescribe massage. Many psychologists will have a personal bias towards some particular theory of psychology and if, for example, their approach happens to stress the influence of childhood trauma on adult behavior, expect to spend a lot of time discussing your early life.

The best way to choose your course of therapy is to do what you feel is best for you.

Trust your instincts, then judge for yourself: if you feel your therapy is working, you are on the right track. If you feel it isn't working, seriously consider changing your therapist.

Others have a perfect right to voice their opinions about what constitutes good therapy but ultimately yours is the only one that matters.

The Tragedy of Misdiagnosis

One young man who was receiving counseling for alcoholism committed suicide and his counselor admitted that he had focused on the man's childhood traumas and family problems in the belief that this was what had caused the youth to turn to drink.

The counselor further admitted that if he had concentrated on the disease of alcoholism, and on getting his patient to stop drinking, all those family problems would probably have disappeared.

Instead, his approach to the counseling sessions had made his patient feel even more depressed.

The young man wasn't able to solve the problems of his childhood or with his family—which never were the real problem anyway—so the loudest message he heard was that he was a failure. This perception led to more intense feelings of depression, more frequent bouts of drinking, more depression, more drinking... until the situation became more than the unfortunate young man could tolerate. He took his own life.

The case illustrates an important point: A correct diagnosis is essential to the successful treatment of any condition.

If you have been emotionally raped but are led into discussing issues that prevent you from addressing the trauma of that experience, or which make you feel like a failure, you could be adding an unnecessary element of risk to your recovery.

The victim of emotional rape needs to be treated like a rape victim. Any problems you are having at this time are most probably the result of the traumatic aftermath, not the other way around.

Confidentiality and Compromise

One woman who was emotionally raped by her husband had her treatment records, which were held by her psychiatrist and psychologist, subpoenaed by his attorney.

The attorney argued that this was justified and necessary because the woman was on medical disability, which affected spousal support and made her medical treatment an issue in the divorce proceedings.

Clearly, the fact that it is possible to call personal therapy records in evidence in such situations may have the effect of restricting the free communication between counselor and patient. Nevertheless, it is the case, and emotional rape victims need to be aware that their medical records, even those recording extremely personal counseling sessions, are not necessarily confidential.

Although very few, if any, therapists would release records without the written permission of the patient, circumstances can be such that it is difficult, if not impossible, to deny permission.

In a divorce, for example, where questions of spousal

support arise there is always a risk that the court will not look favorably upon the party who decides not to sign such a release. Certainly, the State, the Social Security office, and an employer's insurance company would probably insist on access to medical records before qualifying someone for medical disability.

These considerations should not deter you from seeking the help you need to help you recover. Ultimately, the top priority is your emotional well-being. However, knowing the legal situation, you can take your own precautions:

■ Phrase carefully everything you say to your doctor, psychiatrist, or psychologist, so that what is recorded will be in your best interests, not the interests of your rapist.

■ You might also request that certain things not be put into your medical record, or that no written records be kept at all. There is no law compelling a therapist to keep written records, indeed many whose cases are particularly sensitive deliberately avoid doing so.

'People Power'

Earlier, we identified our built-in tendency to interpret the facts in our own favor, often despite all the evidence. Twelve-step programs effectively counteract this sometimes dangerous inclination, focusing on the values of honesty, good judgment and awareness of our own weaknesses—all of which are useful for preventing another emotional rape in the future.

They also prove the benefits of "people power." One emotional rape victim, a recovered alcoholic, said that just having the companionship of the other people in her Alcoholics Anonymous group had made an enormous difference. She spent a lot of time simply talking with others over coffee, and the mere fact that someone listened without charging her a huge hourly fee restored her faith in human nature.

However, she also recalled parts of the twelve-step philosophy that she couldn't agree with, but had to tolerate. For example, she was advised to make amends with her rapist for allowing him to emotionally rape her; a suggestion she ignored. Be aware that twelve-step programs do tend to encourage the acceptance of blame.

Finally, consider that you will significantly help your own recovery if you can reach out and help another victim of emotional rape.

You may not feel able to do this straight away, nor should you force yourself to do so. However, wait until it feels right, then why not start your own support group?

Get in Touch Through Religion

The primary purpose of religion is not to put people in touch with God, but to put them in touch with each other.

—Harold Kushner, *Who Needs God?*

Just as twelve-step programs bring people together, which helps the healing process, so religion can also play a part in recovery.

If you have a formal religion, do not overlook it as a way to muster additional support.

Talk with your minister, priest, or rabbi about what has happened and how you are feeling. Ask for suggestions about ways your religion or church could help. Many churches have their own programs to help people get through times of stress and trauma, and may also organize social activities.

However, as with twelve-step programs, be alert for well-meaning comments and judgments that foster feelings of self-blame.

One man, who was emotionally raped by his wife, recalled that even though his more religious friends did not directly blame him for what happened they repeatedly made comments like "A strong marriage needs a strong religious faith"—the implication being that the marriage had failed because somehow God had been excluded. He felt that in some way these friends held him responsible.

Memos on Recovery 9

Using These Checklists

What follows is a point-by-point guide to recovery, a brief summary of the previous four chapters intended as a quick checklist to aid the transformation of emotional rape victims into emotional rape survivors.

In fact, there are two checklists, both presented as memos for future use. The first is addressed to the victim/survivor; the second, no less important, to his or her friends and family, whose understanding and support can help enormously in the recovery process.

Neither memo is intended as a substitute for reading and re-reading the rest of this book as often as time allows. If you are a victim turn to them when you need reassurance, clarification and validation of your feelings and a few minutes is all the time you have.

Keep a bookmark always at this page. Or photocopy the memos—enlarge them into mini-posters if you wish—so even if you can't carry this book everywhere, you can always have these reminders with you, ready when you need them...

Memo...
to the Victim—Turned Survivor

- Emotional rape is a powerful experience. Recovery will not be without pain or effort and it will take time. Just as a butterfly struggles to escape its cocoon, you can expect to be transformed when you emerge as a survivor.

- **Have faith...that there is more to life than meets the eye—and that there is meaning and purpose to what you are going through, even if you can't yet see what that meaning and purpose is.**

- Have faith...that the emotional pain you are experiencing exists to protect you and that it will not last forever. Visualize your own recovery and the recovery of others.

- **Have faith...that you will recover, and that you don't have to understand how.**

- If you have been emotionally raped you need to treat yourself like a rape victim. Acknowledge that evil exists and that you didn't do anything morally wrong. Don't deny what happened. Be thankful that it wasn't worse.

- **Know what to expect from yourself and others, if for no other reason than to know that you are not going insane and that your emotional wounds will heal. Don't ever consider taking any permanent solutions to what are, after all, temporary problems. Be willing to recover.**

- Accept that you were, and are, powerless to resist the HALF factors: Health, Achievement, Love, and Faith. They are fundamental, built-in human needs.

- **Know that you are not responsible for your powerlessness. You are only responsible for the choices you make to satisfy your powerlessness, not for the choices of others.**

- Your ability to love and trust has not been taken away permanently. You generated the love and trust before, and you will do so again—when you are ready. The next time, it will be for the right people and the right reasons.

- **Keep your sense of humor and be prepared to take small steps forward towards full recovery. Moving forward just a little at a time is still moving forward.**

- Channel the anger, rage, and pain which you will feel in the aftermath of emotional rape in a positive direction. Take full advantage of this abundant source of energy.

- **Go into action. Get started on a regular program of exercise. Eat healthy foods. Stay away from alcohol, drugs, food—anything which, when indulged in to excess, provides only temporary relief but has lasting ill-effects on your physical and mental well-being.**

- Be nice to yourself. Take time out to relax whenever you can, even if only for a few minutes during a busy day. If possible get away on a restful vacation.

- **Try to communicate your feelings to others. Explore the possibilities of professional counseling. If you feel able, extend a helping hand to others who are trying to recover.**

- Finally, always remember these inspiring words of Dr. Elisabeth Kubler-Ross:

  "If you face a problem, whether you are able to solve it or not, you will grow."

  "If we really want to live, we must have the courage to recognize that life is ultimately very short and that everything we do counts."

Memo...
to Friends and Family

If you have a friend or loved one who was a victim of emotional rape, you can help in the recovery process:

- Love them.

- **Be trustworthy, loyal, and dependable.**

- Believe what they tell you.

- **Listen.**

- Comfort them and—above all—do not blame them.

- **Protect them. Don't let them injure themselves still further by using alcohol or drugs, or let them get into debt or pursue other forms of self-destructive behavior. Try to make sure they take sufficient time before getting into another serious relationship.**

- Help them choose a good counselor and doctor.

- **If legal issues are involved, help them to find a good attorney.**

- Help organize information so they can make good decisions for themselves. Offer carefully considered advice, but don't try to make all their decisions for them.

- **Be available. Don't believe them when they say they are okay.**

  Go out of your way to see them, whether or not they appear to want your company. Give them some space, if that's what they want, but don't let them isolate themselves completely.

- Learn what to expect from them by reading Chapter Two of this book, which looks at the aftermath of emotional rape. Don't react negatively or uncaringly to their changes of mood.

- **Be patient—recovery takes time.**

- Make sure they are being good to themselves; eating the right foods and getting enough exercise.

- **Acknowledge yourself for being a good friend and for loving and caring about others.**

Changing Focus:
the Wider Angle   10

Macro Forces

Society transmits the cultural component of human nature, and thereby modifies the individual.
—Anthony Walsh, *Human Nature and Love.*

To understand all the factors that contribute to emotional rape we have to examine the macro forces that shape individual behavior, the powerful influences that determine the nature of the cultural baggage we all carry with us in our daily lives.

These forces have a tremendous, often unacknowledged, impact on our personal value systems, a fact recognized by many authors of books on sexual rape, who discuss how certain aspects of our culture promote and sanction sexual rape or the male domination of women.

There are numerous examples proving this argument. In *I Never Called It Rape* author Robin Warshaw recalls the moment in the television series *Moonlighting* when Cybill Shepherd and Bruce Willis finally had sex.

It is unlikely that many people were surprised or

shocked by those scenes. However, they were horrifying to certain viewers. The scenes involved name-calling, slapping, and falling furniture—perpetuating the notion that women, even intelligent and successful women, enjoy a certain amount of physical violence in their sexual relations. The viewers horrified by this insidious televisual suggestion were women who had been sexually raped.

Such implicit messages are nothing new. Consider the famous scene from *Gone With The Wind* in which Rhett Butler ignores the protests of Scarlett O'Hara and sweeps her off her feet, up the staircase and, we are obviously meant to believe, into the bedroom.

Coming up to date, the film *Basic Instinct* includes steamy sex scenes in which the leading male, a detective played by Michael Douglas, rips off his girlfriend's underwear.

There is little value in seeking to apportion blame. It is more useful to illustrate the extreme difficulty, if not impossibility, of isolating the morality of the individual from the values of the social whole.

High-Tech Influences

At some level a television executive must have made a value judgment about whether that particular scene in the *Moonlighting* series was acceptable for the TV audience—a decision about its overall cultural message. That value judgment influenced the beliefs, attitudes and possibly the behavior of millions of individuals, to a degree that is impossible to calculate.

An excellent example of the interplay between individual behavior and social acceptability is the dramatic change in social attitudes towards smoking in recent years. One man who had smoked cigarettes for over thirty years explained why he finally kicked the habit:

"It's just too much of a hassle to smoke now. You can't

do it in restaurants, on airplanes, at business meetings, in the work place, theaters...I know I'd never stop if it was accepted the way it used to be, but you're really in the minority if you smoke nowadays."

He went on to reminisce about the old movies, like *Casablanca*, which romanticized smoking and drinking. It was as if his addictive side was longing for the "good old days," when society sanctioned his addiction.

Simply stated, society can have a significant impact upon the values of the individual, and vice versa. This is especially, and increasingly, true in this age of burgeoning high-technology mass communications.

The macro forces that sanction and facilitate emotional rape are extremely subtle, very much like the romanticizing of smoking and drinking in *Casablanca*, and being aware of these forces makes victims less likely to blame themselves for what happened or to accept blame from others. (This awareness also plays an important role in any effective self-defense plan.)

Until now emotional rape has been examined primarily from the standpoint of the individual: we've looked in detail at case histories, at what distinguishes an emotional rape relationship, at the traumatic aftereffects, at what makes emotional rape possible, and at how victims can recover to become survivors.

The three following chapters, on Society, Medicine and The Law, change the focus to consider emotional rape in a broader context.

These chapters are about recognizing that these powerful, macro forces are at work in our society, and demonstrating that we should all be actively concerned about what beliefs, attitudes, and patterns of behavior they encourage.

Society 11

The TV Age

The most powerful influences on society's values are those exerted by the mass media: music and the cinema, newspapers and magazines, and particularly television.

No television producer would ever consider screening a "How To..." program on child molestation. Molesting children is not acceptable in our society, it is not acceptable to promote such behavior, and those TV programs that do tackle the subject emphasize that it is a detestable crime.

However, what about a "How To..." show on emotional rape, perhaps subtitled "How to Use Love to Get Money" or "How to Marry Rich"?

In fact, the second such title *was* chosen for one of the Phil Donahue shows, and the special guest was a woman who gave workshops on how to marry into money. The show featured some of her students, all females, and the audience learned how their mentor had even taken them on "field trips" in search of rich men. References to the place of love and mutual respect in the marriage relationship were rare; the important thing was that one chose a partner for his (it could just as well have been "her") money.

Never mind that someone obviously deemed this theme suitable for any sort of televised airing, Donahue also enthusiastically advertised a cassette tape called "How to Marry Rich."

When some of the studio audience voiced negative opinions about this approach to marriage, Donahue responded with lighthearted rhetorical questions such as: "Isn't it as easy to love a rich person as it is a poor one?" In other words, he seemed to sanction the entire idea, and encouraged his audience to do the same.

Of course, the media cannot be held wholly responsible for society's values. People like Donahue produce what sells, that's their job, and as much as shows like Donahue's *shape* our values, the topics they choose and the way they present them *reflect* our values—what is, and what is not, acceptable to us.

As a society we demand that certain topics be presented in certain ways. The molesting of children is just one example: it is unlikely that Donahue could influence any audience to respond favorably to child molestation, indeed he would surely jeopardize his career if he were even to attempt such an exercise. However, we are not as particular about other, extremely damaging, areas of behavior, such as emotional rape.

How can we protect ourselves or others from emotional rape if we are immersed in values that seem not only to sanction, but also to encourage it?

Popular Music

Ideally, popular culture would validate each one of us, not just those who are in a good relationship and have everything they want. This doesn't happen. Instead, we are relentlessly assaulted by messages telling us we are not okay unless we have a special person, or a particular thing, in our lives.

It is no exaggeration to say that the lyrics to ninety percent of popular songs, for example, tell us we're not going to be happy without someone or something, and those who have had a catchy tune run repeatedly through their minds will readily appreciate the subtle power such music can exercise over our moods and attitudes.

Because we are also powerless to resist our built-in needs for love and achievement, this constant "brainwashing" imparts an unnecessary urgency to our search for that special person or thing—often with the result that having *someone* becomes more important than *who* we have.

As we saw in the case of Iris and Mark, recounted in Chapter Eight, being married was more important to Iris than the character of the person she was marrying.

Morality and the Movies

Popular films don't always make a very positive contribution to our value system either.

The movie *Pretty Woman*, for example, is about a prostitute whose sex appeal and personality enable her to gain the love of a wealthy man. It was a none-too-imaginative reworking of the old, and enduringly popular, Cinderella theme.

An implicit assumption of this theme is that the achievement of material wealth, initially at least through physical, superficial attractiveness, is an acceptable foundation for a lasting relationship. Broken down, the initial exchange between the two partners could involve the illusion of love, or sex, for money. In the case of *Pretty Woman* the formula resulted in a remarkable box-office success.

However, was it absolutely necessary for the female character to be a prostitute? Could the film have worked just as well, or even better, if she had been a waitress or a homeless woman selling newspapers, resisting the readily available and more lucrative avenue of prostitution? The answer would be yes—if it were not for society's continued fascination with the sex/love-for-money relationship.

Popular culture feeds this fascination in the interest of producing films/TV programs/magazines/songs that are popular and will therefore make a handsome profit.

These fascinations steadily become a more established part of society's value system, increasingly difficult to dislodge from the mass consciousness.

Repeating the Lie

Unfortunately, dubious moral messages are endemic in modern mass culture. Talk shows almost daily provide the most breathtaking instances of banality of topic and irresponsibility of treatment. Even children's cartoons are not above criticism.

Consider how one episode of the Alvin and the Chipmunks cartoon was about Alvin's schoolboy crush on his grade school teacher, a tall, attractive blonde.

Daydreaming at his desk, Alvin imagined himself opening his billfold and money just pouring out, enabling him to pay for a romantic boat ride. During the ride he reached into his pocket, pulled out a ring box, and out burst a diamond ring, considerably bigger than the box itself. At this point in the cartoon, hearts of love flowed from the teacher as she hugged Alvin and kissed him. The message, quite clearly, was that you can buy love.

This is certainly not a farfetched example, rather it is an excellent illustration of how dubious cultural messages operate on all levels, and with a dangerous subtlety.

The script-writer who plotted the course of Alvin's cartoon dream probably wasn't even aware of the message he was creating. He simply drew on one of those oft-repeated, almost mythical, misconceptions—that having money can ensure you have love—and reworked that old theme, thereby consolidating its cultural position.

It was the creative process without any real creativity being involved; it had all been done before, countless times, by TV producers, writers, film directors and song-writers.

Therein lies the most worrying characteristic of modern culture: there is so little awareness of the existence, and power, of these macro forces that we're seldom even aware that we are affected by them. Moreover, we can't begin to change them until we can identify them.

Dishonesty on Demand

Like the air we breathe, dishonesty is all around us. We are so bombarded with obvious lies that we are immune to them; we have been numbed into non-perception.

In the hyperbole of advertising, do things really go better with Coke? Has anyone yet seen a 'thousand points of light'? Are Pop Tarts really a good adult breakfast?

Do we care at all?

The reality doesn't seem to matter anymore. Dishonesty has promoted more dishonesty, which has promoted more... until dishonesty has finally become institutionalized.

For those whose livelihoods depend on being able to manipulate public opinion—the creators of those slick advertising campaigns, for instance—there is a golden rule: if you don't match dishonesty with even more blatant dishonesty, you lose. We believed things went better with Coke. Inevitably, the opposition had to create the Pepsi Generation. In reality, the nutritional value of either soft drink is questionable.

The world of politics is also a fine example. Throughout the 1980s anyone who tried to remind us of the unpalatable truth that we were living beyond our means, creating an economic time bomb for the years to come (the national debt), was generally banished to the political wilderness; a party-pooper in an orgy of plenty.

However, politics is only a mirror reflecting society's numbed values. We didn't want to hear what we didn't want to hear; so our leaders, whose jobs depend on their popular appeal, didn't tell us. Who can really blame them?

Politicians do what they have to do to get elected, and stay elected, just as advertisers do what they have to do to sell their products. It is society that elects the politicians and buys the products. If we want these people to tell us that everything is going to be all right, or if we are willing to believe that things do go better with Coke, then so be it.

Dishonesty, a key tool of the emotional rapist, has become so commonplace that we have become immune to the common signals that warn us when dishonesty is near. Indeed, we are not only immune to it, we demand it, making us all more vulnerable.

The Education System

The truth is that schools don't really teach anything except to obey orders. Our education system is just a more cosmetic way to create dependent human beings, unable to fill their own hours, unable to initiate lines of meaning to give substance and pleasure to their existence.

Think of the things that are killing us as a nation: drugs, brainless competition, recreational sex, the pornography of violence, gambling, alcohol, and the worst pornography of all—lives devoted to buying things, accumulation as a philosophy. All are addictions of dependent personalities, and that is what our brand of schooling must inevitably produce.

—John Gatto, New York State Teacher of The Year, 1991.

Our education system encourages a mind set that is perfect for emotional rape: unquestioning, addictive and materialistic. From the very beginning we are taught to accept and maintain the status quo; to believe what we are told, not taught to question.

The lesson quickly learned by any student inclined to think independently and question the "facts" as presented by teaching staff is that all he or she will achieve is a lower grade. The key to success in school is to memorize what the teacher says is the correct answer, and never to challenge this basic, unwritten rule.

As young people leave the education system, become adults and join the world of work, they take these attitudes with them, so that the climate for emotional rape permeates every area of our society. It is worth remembering that emotional rape does not only occur in intimate, one-on-one relationships; it can also occur between employee and employer, and in other situations.

In Praise of Incompetence

This formative, addictive system sets the pattern for our adult lives.

As noted by Anne Wilson Schaef and Diane Fassel (*When Society Becomes an Addict,* and *The Addictive Organization*), society has reached the point where skilled incompetence is valued more highly in the workplace than true competence.

We are no longer at all surprised to witness some high-ranking corporate executive "answering" specific questions, apparently with complete candor—but saying nothing. The ability to misinform and hide the truth has become a valued and sought-after executive skill.

Schaef and Fassel identify true competence as the ability to know and identify the truth, and to make things right. However the truly competent, like the engineers who questioned the safety of the Challenger spacecraft's O-rings, are viewed and treated as whistle-blowers. They are not what the system calls "team players," hence they are not desirable employees and are likely to be branded mavericks or "loose cannons."

The nuclear engineer Peter Faulkner is a celebrated case in point.

Faulkner was working for one of the major nuclear reactor companies when he agreed to testify at Congressional hearings on nuclear power, with the understanding that the government would protect him from any reprisals by his employers. However, after the hearings his company laid him off at the first opportunity and, not surprisingly, he was unable to get another job in the industry.

In the early days of his unemployment he edited a book called *The Silent Bomb* that concisely and correctly identified many of the major problems with nuclear power, years before the accidents at Three Mile Island or Chernobyl. As well as providing a warning of the potential for tragedy in the nuclear power industry, the book was Faulkner's attempt to regain some degree of legitimacy and professional respectability.

However, although the validity of his observations was proven years later, at the time his efforts singularly failed to revive his career.

Even after the disasters at Three Mile Island and Chernobyl, he was reduced to living on a friend's porch because that was the only accommodation he could afford on his earnings as a ski instructor.

It is a story that should concern us all. A perceptive, experienced, expert in a vital high-technology field had been ruined, his skills lost to society, just because he had the courage to speak the truth as he saw it.

Creating the Climate for Rape

Faulkner's fate is a classic example of how the addictive system fostered by our society can turn courage and competence into failure—with the result that we have a difficult time distinguishing dishonesty from virtue.

Inevitably, the emotional rapist is able to operate almost with impunity in such favorable conditions. Our toleration and encouragement of an addictive, materialistic value system creates a social climate where the tools of the emotional rapist—attraction, dishonesty and manipulation—are not only accepted, but may be widely-admired, even respected.

When executives, for example, are being paid huge salaries to evade the truth, is it any wonder that the public mind begins to associate deception with competence, or some type of positive personal virtue?

Is it any wonder, in a society with an education system which teaches us not to question the status quo, that certain people become emotional rapists, or that the rest of us might be vulnerable to their evil intentions?

The truly competent people who value honesty and decency, and have an instinct to do "the right thing," are *extremely* vulnerable.

They are immersed in a system that teaches us that dishonesty, manipulation, incompetence, misinformation and distortion are good, while honesty and competence are bad; a system that makes sure the emotional rapist is unlikely to stand out in the crowd.

The Lesson That 'Anything Goes'

In those states where the officially approved explanation for the origin of life is based on the Darwinian theory of evolution, our public education system also underpins the notion that life has no meaning or purpose.

Evolutionary theory diminishes the possibility that there may be something more to human existence than is superficially evident; what we see and know of life is all there is, and therefore must be all-important. Humanity should not concern itself with what we can never really know—acknowledgment of a Greater Power, or Creative Force, for example—because in Darwinian terms what you see is what you get.

Unfortunately, the frequent lesson learned from this is that "anything goes." We might as well get what we can, while we can, and pay the lowest price possible, whatever the moral implications.

One anthropology professor at Rutgers University studied student cheating and concluded that it had become "an academic skill almost as important as reading, writing, and math." Another academic engaged in similar study found that "there is definitely a climate in which students feel it's okay to do whatever they need to do to get grades." She linked the cheating to "materialism."

Teaching by Poor Example

Evolutionary theory is not only a chaotic foundation for a moral value system, it is also extremely dubious science.

As discussed earlier, the probability of life originating or evolving by random chance is about as close to zero as it is possible to imagine. Furthermore, selecting evolution as the only "approved" explanation of life is poor science, ruling out other, equally plausible, explanations such as the existence of a Higher Intelligence.

The need to keep an open mind whenever possible has always been recognized by the greatest scientists, and remembering such wisdom is never more important than when formulating theories that are fundamental to the meaning and purpose of our very existence.

The theory of evolution should not be replaced with

creationism, rather both points of view should be given equal time and emphasis in our classrooms. That's not only good science, but good education and a better foundation for a positive value system.

It is precisely because our schools provide the foundations for society's future that it is essential to focus at length on the education system. If those foundations include meaninglessness, society's values are unlikely to be healthy and positive, unlikely to be capable of recognizing evil and negative behavior.

Exchanging the Lie

If society fails to acknowledge powerlessness, it has to assume that the victims of emotional rape are weak, lack intelligence, or somehow chose what happened to them. And there is a subconscious agreement to exchange the lie that we are all in control, which is a dangerous state of affairs.

First, we have no power to resist the HALF factors (Health, Achievement, Love, and Faith), but in believing that we do, we are bound to be off guard if any of these factors is exploited.

Second, as long as we believe we are in control, we tend to feel we are wholly responsible for what happens to us. This is only one step away from believing there's no such thing as emotional rape, and it is denying the existence of emotional rape that helps make it possible.

If we believe we are able to control everything that happens in our lives, instead of seeing emotional rape for what it is—the self-serving misuse of the best instinctive human qualities, such as love and trust—we see it as a natural and unavoidable aspect of life.

There is absolutely no reason why we should accept this as a valid view; it obviously isn't accepted as valid when applied to other areas of human behavior.

We would never suggest that child molestation is natural and unavoidable. Instead, we accept that children are powerless, and that the child molester is evil. The only reason we do not apply the same logical process to consideration of emotional rape is because we believe the silent lie that we are strong and in control.

Society does not appreciate the full range of powerlessness. We need to acknowledge our powerlessness to resist the HALF factors in the same way that we concede the inherent vulnerability of a child.

The Potential for Evil—in Us All

The potential for evil exists in all of us; in ourselves, our parents, our neighbors, our children, our spouse, our closest friends. However, we fear that if we admit this we will no longer be holy, divine, or immortal, and that nothing will matter. To protect ourselves, we deny all but the most blatant and hideous instances of evil, instances that distinguish "them" from "us," and in the long-term we become desensitized to acts of evil.

For example, a television news report revealed how student protesters were tortured and pushed to their deaths from helicopters for opposing the brutal regime of a South American dictator.

In one particularly harrowing story, a militiaman poured gasoline on a young girl and set her on fire. The report went on to discuss the evil of the dictator. However, the fundamental question raised by the report, one that demanded an answer, wasn't to do with the evil of the dictator (it was not the dictator himself, after all, who killed the girl). It was, How could one human being set another innocent and helpless human being on fire? To answer this, we must admit the unpalatable truth that the potential for evil exists in every one of us.

Stalin didn't exterminate twenty million people by

himself. Hitler didn't perpetrate the Holocaust on his own. Their evil agendas were carried out with the help and co-operation of many thousands of people. These are only two examples from recent history, there are many others.

The exploitation of humankind's inherent potential for evil is not a rare occurrence.

Embarrassing Admissions

If we are to study the nature of human evil, it is doubtful how clearly we will be able to separate them from us; it will most likely be our own natures we are examining. Undoubtedly, this potential for (self-) embarrassment is one of the reasons we have thus far failed to develop a psychology of evil.

—Dr. M. Scott Peck, *The People of The Lie.*

We must see evil as something that affects each one of us. Like a virus, it is dangerously infectious and damaging to all human life.

Unfortunately, though, many of us don't want to pull anyone else's covers because we might expose ourselves. In our unwillingness to confront evil we fail to recognize that, like any unchecked virus, it can spread to the point that it becomes endemic in our society; evil acts become the norm, almost socially acceptable.

News bulletins all too frequently tell us how passers-by were able to ignore a victim's screams for help in a mugging or rape attack. Such stories appall us all, yet we somehow manage to avoid facing the truth about evil.

The casualties of emotional rape are just part of the price we pay to avoid addressing the psychology of evil. The payoff is that we don't have to examine our own selves too closely, or risk getting involved.

Medicine 12

Choose Carefully

Survivors of emotional rape need to choose their therapist or psychiatrist carefully—not all mental health professionals share the same views on healing. For example, opinions differ widely over the use of drugs.

Recall Cheryl's story (Chapter Two). She eventually chose to go to a psychologist, after a psychiatrist who saw her in the early stages of her recovery seemed to treat everything with a prescription. It wasn't that the drugs he prescribed were necessarily wrong, or proved ineffective, but Cheryl's personal view was that living in a drug-altered state was not what she needed for her healing process.

The distinction between a therapist who is "drug-oriented" and one who prefers to "talk it out" is easy to recognize. However, there are less obvious differences in approach; differences of emphasis that can be particularly important to survivors.

A Must to Avoid

Therapists to be avoided are those whose approach fosters and sanctions emotional rape and tends to make the victim feel responsible.

Perhaps the best way to demonstrate the damage this type of therapy can inflict is to examine in detail a popular book that champions this type of thinking.

Such a book is *Coming Apart—Why Relationships End and How to Live Through the Ending of Yours,* by Daphne Rose Kingma, a professional psychologist specializing in love and relationships.

Kingma describes thoughts and ideas that could potentially foster and sanction emotional rape, thoughts and ideas that are exactly the same as those that some victims have met with in therapy—and that were counterproductive to their recovery.

(It is acknowledged at the outset that Kingma's book is singled out here purely as a "straw man"; it encompasses and neatly summarizes many of the ideas that are potentially harmful to emotional rape victims. Hers is only one of a number of books espousing similar views; views that are widely accepted and which, in another context perhaps, might have many points to recommend them. However, in cases of emotional rape they are very definitely damaging.)

These excerpts go right to the heart of the matter:

"We don't like to conceive of ourselves as being in a relationship to get something—that's too crass. We don't want to believe that we fall in love in order to get something out of it."

"...the deeper truth is that we all enter into relationships for very specific reasons, whether we choose to see them or not."

"When we fall in love, we fall in love with the person who will help us accomplish something—whether that's something we know we're trying to accomplish, like getting a college degree..."

"...Love is the medium whereby we offer one another this assistance..."

The relative success of her book does not necessarily indicate widespread acceptance of Kingma's views, either by the medical professions or the public. However, it does mean that there must be at least a small number of mental health professionals who agree with her philosophy, one that implicitly sanctions and promotes the use of love to accomplish goals, even blatantly tangible goals such as getting a college degree.

Kingma not only asserts that it is acceptable to use love to get what you want, but that this is normal and emotionally healthy. In her argument it is the victims who are viewed as lacking and unwilling to grow.

Similar Roles, Different Interpretations

One of the case studies outlined in her book is almost identical to the story of Steve and Ellen (Chapter One). Recall that Ellen exploited Steve's love to enable her to embark on an acting career.

In Kingma's study Ted was an established director and Laura was an aspiring actress who, at the outset, feared she might not succeed without someone else's help. After dating for a few months, then living together for a short time, they got married.

As might be expected, Ted's influence helped his wife become established as an actress, but their marriage ended abruptly after Laura landed a role that meant her being away from home for six months.

Kingma explains that Laura had completed her childhood development task of the relationship—evidently to become an actress, or otherwise independent—but that Ted had not outgrown his hidden dependency needs and would therefore have to find another woman to "indulge his ego." Surely an equally plausible interpretation of this situation was that Laura used Ted to advance her acting career, and then the traumatized Ted was told he was in some way responsible.

However else it might be explained in particular cases, using love and marriage because you secretly fear that you may not be able to make it on your own is dishonest.

Kingma does not tell us whether Laura had told Ted the real reason why she was marrying him, but it is doubtful that she did. How many people would marry someone who said what amounted to "I'm marrying you because I fear I can't make it alone, and as soon as I get strong enough I'm going to leave"?

True love is not dishonest, nor self-serving; there are no hidden agendas. Laura used Ted and then, conveniently for her, it was Ted who was told to "grow up."

The 'Forever-Myth'

The idea that love is forever, Kingma also argues, contributes to relationship and marriage problems.

This "forever-myth," she explains, developed when people lived only half as long as they do today; in an age when, according to Kingma, forever meant up to ten years, not the forty to sixty years it could mean today.

But is this valid logic? If anything, our longer life spans make safe and honest relationships all the more important. What is the point of living longer if we don't improve the quality of our lives? (Or are we just prolonging life so we can grow old alone, in constant emotional pain?)

Having it All Ways

Kingma's book also explicitly expresses the belief, frequently encountered among therapists, that everything stems from childhood. She states:

"Even though as adults we know that our childhood experience of safety was an illusion, we want to create a counterpart experience in adulthood by creating loving relationships..."

"...This is also true, in a different way, for people whose parents didn't create a feeling of security in childhood. For them there is a desperate need to establish the sense of security that was always painfully lacking."

This is also a case of having it all ways. If you did have a safe childhood environment, you're trying to recreate it; if you didn't, you're trying to create it for the first time. Obviously, if we accept this approach all relationship problems must stem from childhood because everyone must have had either a safe or an unsafe childhood. It's *Catch-22* logic that denies the reality of love.

Psychiatrist Dr. Theodore Isaac Rubin observes in his book *Real Love* that:

Our need for love is as great as our need to breathe and it does for our psyches and inner selves what clean air does for our lungs.

Love is as real and necessary as the air we breathe. And adults need air just as much as children do. We didn't make it that way, that's just the way it is, and the reason there are now so many divorces and relationship problems isn't because we have failed to understand that love is a myth, it's because we believe the over-told lie that it is.

We have no respect for the reality and sanctity of love, so we continue to misuse it.

When people enter into a relationship solely to achieve something for themselves it is inevitable that the relationship will end when that goal is attained

and there is a very strong possibility that one of the parties involved will be traumatized by the experience.

If love was intended to be the currency of personal advancement, then surely feeling used by someone you love would feel good. But it most certainly doesn't, which might be seen as Nature's way of letting us know that using people isn't what life and love is all about.

Just as physical pain tells us when we have our hand on a hot stove, emotional pain tells us that something is not right; that's our own natural warning system.

No Excuses

Certainly there *are* many subtle and complex links between our adult relationships and our childhood experiences. However, this does not enable those who act with evil intent to abdicate responsibility for their actions, just as it does not place the burden of responsibility upon the innocent party who falls prey to them.

Society doesn't excuse a burglar because he was trying to steal something he once had, or didn't have, in his childhood. It holds that we all have a responsibility to know the difference between good and evil. If for some reason a criminal doesn't know the difference between good and evil, the victim is not turned upon and told to "grow up," nor is the criminal rewarded for having completed some subtle childhood development task.

There's nothing wrong with Kingma's perception of how love and relationships are exploited and abused in modern society:

Unfortunately, many people do use love and relationships purely for personal gain. However, we identify such exploitation and abuse as emotional rape, not as behavior that is accepted as normal and healthy.

An honest exchange of value-for-value in a relationship isn't emotional rape. If you tell your partner at the outset that you are only entering into marriage to get a college education, for example, and you exchange something of equal value (even if it's only your companionship), that is a fair and honest relationship.

However, the key word is "honest." If you don't tell your partner your true motivation, but operate with a hidden agenda, that is emotional rape.

The Denial of Powerlessness

Kingma's adherence to the notion that everyone is at least partially responsible for everything that happens to them has important implications for the idea of powerlessness.

Recognizing that we are powerless to resist the HALF factors (Health, Achievement, Love, and Faith) is an essential precondition of recovery from emotional rape, just as powerlessness is one of the factors that makes emotional rape possible.

It would be counterproductive to expose any emotional rape survivor to a course of therapy based upon an approach that denies powerlessness.

Recognizing the Paradox

In effect, the acceptance of personal weakness becomes the basis of strength...It is only when the [individual] no longer can maintain the fiction of being in control, when stark reality begins to shatter his illusions, that he is able to set aside his false pride and turn outside himself for support and guidance.

—Dr. Arnold Ludwig, *Understanding the Alcoholic's Mind.*

Those doctors and psychologists who specialize in the treatment of addiction seem to understand powerlessness, and the paradox of recovery, very well. Dr. Ludwig calls the first chapter of his book *Paradoxes and Contradictions.*

However, there are at least some members of the medical profession who are still operating under the illusion that we are in control, and when a survivor of emotional rape encounters one of these healers there is a strong possibility that more damage will be inflicted because the patient will be made to feel like more of a failure.

A Case History

Kingma cites the divorce story of Rosie and Bill, presenting Rosie as having "sabotaged" the marriage by her drinking problem; a woman who turned to alcohol because she could not complete her childhood developmental tasks.

Another explanation, equally valid in psychological terms, might have been that Rosie sabotaged the marriage so she could drink. The key problem may have been her alcoholism, not her failure to complete her childhood developmental tasks. When someone is an alcoholic, they are powerless to resist alcohol; Rosie had no control over what she thought, believed, or perceived.

A therapist's primary objective is to get the emotional rape survivor to see that he or she is powerless in the face of the HALF factors (Health, Achievement, Love, and Faith), that he or she had no chance to resist the rapist's exploitation of these factors—not that he or she was in some way responsible for what happened.

This is one of those paradoxes of recovery: recognizing that you are powerless enables you to move on along the road to recovery, to regain control.

You'll See it When You Believe it

Another notion that contributes to emotional rape and is sometimes found in psychology is an extension of the "bad-call bias"; our tendency to see what we want to see.

Dr. Wayne Dyer, author and psychologist, wrote a self-help program and book, *You'll See It When You Believe It*, that maintains that you have to believe something to make it a reality. Some modern religions, Science of Mind, for example, are also built around this central theme.

Emmet Fox, in his book *The Ten Commandments*, asserts that the North Pole is cold solely because people believe it's cold. Anything is possible, the argument runs, if we think it so; a philosophy that was enthusiastically embraced by the personal growth movement that became popular in the late 1970s and emphasized "creating" or "being" as an avenue to happiness.

Much of such thinking has great merit; people have to believe something is possible before they'll even try to make it happen. But that's not the whole story.

A person might believe that he or she can fly, but it would be a fatal mistake to jump off a tall building. And it would not be wise to "believe," or "create," that a person loves you in order to make this come true. Thinking that you can make someone love you by "believing" they do is the basis for a distorted reality which could make you even more vulnerable to emotional rape.

Belief by itself or taken to extremes can be harmful. Simply believing something is true does not always make it so. Belief has to be applied to the right things.

Blind belief is fundamentally different from making a commitment. We sometimes have to be fully committed to making our personal goals become a reality. However, this commitment should be made only after we are fully informed and have thoroughly examined the situation.

Co-Dependency

The idea of co-dependency originated from the treatment of alcoholism, the underlying belief being that people who surround an alcoholic subconsciously support him or her in his or her drinking. For example, if the wife of an alcoholic telephones his boss for him and says he has influenza when he is suffering from a hangover, she is participating in the denial that there's a problem with alcohol.

Without doubt the concept is a valid one, however as addiction becomes more generalized so does co-dependency. We now recognize addicts to sex, relationships, food, power, control, gambling, romance, work, money... therefore, by definition we have to recognize there are co-dependents to all these addictions.

If you have been emotionally raped, it is likely that your therapist will talk to you about addictive relationships. You may be asked to consider the possibility that you are a co-dependent and somehow contributed to your own dilemma.

However, while there is a time and place for examining co-dependency, that time and place may not be in the immediate treatment of emotional rape.

Always keep in mind that there is a limit to the responsibilities of co-dependents; a rape victim is not a co-rapist, a murder victim is not a co-murderer, a molested child is not a co-molester.

When someone falls victim to evil, making him or her feel responsible only makes the situation worse. Constructive rape therapy emphasizes that the victim is not responsible.

The Law   13

The Burden of Proof

Brent methodically exploited two women, Barbara and Shara (Chapter Three), and it's certain these were cases of emotional rape because he was incriminated by the telephone messages Shara left on his answering machine.

The seriousness of Brent's actions was also tragically evident: Shara took her own life by jumping from a freeway overpass into the rush hour traffic.

However, neither the victims nor their families had any obvious legal recourse against him. If they attempted to sue him they would probably lose the case and find themselves being countersued for damages. Brent would swear that he truly loved both women, and that the relationships failed for reasons that were beyond his control. Legally, it could not be proved otherwise.

No Fault—No Protection...

In most of the United States there is no legal protection against emotional rape in marriage.

Most states have "no-fault" divorce laws that mean the partners' behavior is not considered in the proceedings; the law is simply concerned with the legal dissolution of the marriage, not with who may or may not have been at fault in the breakup.

One example of the no-fault principle in action: a male victim of emotional rape discovered that his wife had an abortion and might have been pregnant when they separated. He had a vasectomy six years earlier, so could not have been the father, but because they lived in a no-fault state he could not even mention the abortion in the divorce proceedings.

His attorney's memorable legal opinion was: "She could have slept with the entire US Navy and it still wouldn't make any difference." Only nine states consider adultery suitable grounds for divorce, and hence allowable in legal proceedings.

...No Justice

No-fault divorce opens up a huge number of opportunities for the emotional rapist because most states also have community property laws which maintain that anything gained or lost during marriage is a joint debt or asset. Ostensibly this is a reasonable and fair assumption. In reality, it's a principle that can be exploited and abused.

Shortly after getting married to Jason, Jenny used most of her own savings to buy a condominium. Two years later she discovered she had been emotionally raped by her husband but, because she was married to him when she bought the property, he was able to claim half of its value as his own personal asset.

This was not the only loss Jenny incurred. Unbeknown to her, Jason had also run up considerable debts by paying for his business expenses with a credit card, then pocketing the money when his company reimbursed him.

Jenny had no knowledge of this extra money, nor how it had been used, but she was held liable to pay half of the credit card debts because they were deemed community in nature.

Her two-year marriage cost her nearly $50,000.

Fertile Grounds for Rape

Many states also have "public policies" regarding marriage. In some states, for example, it is against public policy to waive spousal support before marriage because, it is argued, such a waiver would encourage infidelity—presumably by the male—in the future.

However, even if we accept this public policy has the effect of strengthening the institution of marriage, we have to admit that it can also result in considerable miscarriages of justice.

If spousal support cannot be waived before marriage, by drawing up a prenuptial agreement, any subsequent divorce action will always favor the spouse with the lower income. Even in short marriages with no children involved, spousal support is typically awarded on algebraic formulas that consider only the gross incomes of the parties.

Such laws make marriage fertile ground for emotional rapists.

They can use love to marry someone with greater assets and/or a higher income than their own and will almost certainly emerge better off when the relationship ends in divorce:

■ Any savings accrued during the marriage are split equally, even if the money came solely from the wage packet of the higher-income victim.

■ The liability for any debts is also shared equally, even if those debts were incurred solely by the emotional rapist.

■ The lower-income partner, the emotional rapist, will probably be awarded spousal support.

It's all perfectly legal—although it doesn't seem as if it should be.

Debbie vs. Andrew

Debbie's priest told her he had a very personable nephew, Andrew, who lived in central Europe. She traveled to meet Andrew, fell in love, and eventually they got married. Both of them wanted to live in the United States, so she completed the necessary immigration papers for Andrew and they moved back to her home town.

Then her world fell apart.

Just two weeks after their arrival Andrew announced his hidden agenda: he had only married her to obtain visas to live and work in the United States. He said he found her unattractive and boring, and moved into a church monastery where his uncle was a priest.

The marriage was never consummated in the USA and for three years Debbie has been trying, without success, to get the marriage annulled. In fact, Andrew reported her to the authorities for not supporting him as she had agreed to in the immigration declarations.

The law ignores the obvious deception perpetrated by Andrew to gain entry into the United States; indeed, it penalizes rather than protects victims such as Debbie.

David vs. Goliath

The outlook for victims is not always entirely bleak, however; success or failure in the courtroom depends upon the nature of the rapist involved.

The explosion on the battleship Iowa in the late-1980s,

in which many sailors lost their lives, was described by the Navy as a murder/suicide with a homosexual love triangle at the core. The alleged murderer was identified as a seaman called Ken Hartwig.

But according to one media report into the incident, naval intelligence investigators intimidated witnesses into making statements that implicated Seaman Hartwig. Among other things, it was implied by the investigators that Hartwig's wife had sex with his Navy friends. Moreover, a detailed investigation, by Congress, failed to substantiate the Navy's explanation for the explosion and found evidence of potential negligence and a lack of training by the Navy.

The true victims were Seaman Hartwig, his family and the other casualties. The Navy simply used his patriotism, loyalty and sense of duty, as well as his friendships with other sailors, in an attempt to camouflage their own negligence and incompetence.

His family is suing the Navy for wrongful infliction of emotional distress and has a reasonable chance of winning their case.

In one-on-one legal battles with an emotional rapist there is seldom any chance that the victim will gain a fair settlement.

In David versus Goliath situations, however, when the rapist is a large corporation or an institution such as the government, there is a chance that the victim will triumph.

Self-Defense 14

Caution and Commonsense

We cannot protect ourselves completely against emotional rape. To guarantee such immunity we would have to stop loving and trusting others altogether.

We would have to exclude all higher emotions from our lives, which would be rather like holding our breath to avoid air pollution; the "means" would be far too damaging to justify the "ends." We would commit emotional suicide, or risk becoming totally paranoid.

Living life to the full involves risk-taking and this chapter is about reducing those risks—specifically those attendant upon any worthwhile relationship with another human being. For the survivor it is about protecting yourself as much as possible to avoid having to go through the same awful trauma a second time; about returning without fear to a life that includes love and trust.

Much of the advice is simply commonsense, much of it has been mentioned in passing in previous chapters. However, this is the first time all our "precautionary tales" have been brought together and this "concentration" may give the impression that to avoid being emotionally raped we have to lose all spontaneity, romance and instinctive love in our relationships; that feelings have to be buried under the weight of analysis, legal advice, prenuptial agreements and financial planning. This is not the case.

This emphasis is simply unavoidable. Any discussion of self-defense strategies has to focus on practical, cold considerations.

The intent throughout this book is to affirm all that is good in human relationships and to affirm the marvelous experiences that are possible when we base those relationships on honesty, mutual respect and fulfillment of our higher emotions.

Check Out the Pool Before Diving In

Protecting yourself is more a matter of adopting a certain philosophy and way of life than of measuring each relationship against a set list of requirements. It is a matter of:

- not ignoring the obvious;
- recognizing that you are powerless to resist the HALF factors (Health, Achievement, Love, and Faith);
- being honest with yourself;
- trusting your own intuition;
- avoiding obviously dangerous situations;
- not compromising your own system of values.

This is not advocating paranoia, it's merely suggesting that it makes good sense to check that there *is* water in the pool before diving in.

(In the interests of brevity and simplicity what follows focuses on self-defense in one-on-one relationships, but the same advice applies equally to other situations where an individual might be at risk.)

Look Behind the Mask

Physical appearances don't help you tell whether a person is an emotional rapist. In fact such people are invariably charming, attractive personalities on the surface; these qualities are important tools to a rapist. Potential rapists have to be identified by looking behind the mask—by examining their true character rather than accepting them, quite literally, at face value.

Don't Ignore the Obvious

"Looking back, were there clues that might have warned you about the type of person your rapist was?"
"Oh yes, there were warning signs all over the place, I just didn't pay any attention to them. I thought things would be different with me."
Every victim of emotional rape interviewed for this book was asked the same question; without fail, every one gave something like the same answer. The explanation for this is simple: our vested interests interfere with our perception.

We see what we want to see, believe what we want to believe:
- We want to believe that the ones we love also love us.
- We want to believe our hard work, achievement and sacrifice will be appreciated.
- We want to believe in fair play and loyalty.
- We want to believe the tennis ball hit the line (remember the "bad-call bias," our tendency to believe that the ball always falls in our own favor?).

Occasionally we want so much to believe certain things that it interferes with our perception of the way they really are. We are faced with a balancing act: On one hand, it's important to have a positive attitude towards our personal and professional relationships. In a sense, we have to believe the best of a situation; being paranoid quickly takes its own toll. On the other hand, we have to be sure that our need to see things a certain way is not distorting reality.

This isn't to say that those victims who ignored all the warning signs about their rapist should be held responsible for what happened to them. They are not. It's just that they owe it to themselves to make sure it doesn't happen again.

Don't Judge With the Benefit of Hindsight

Understanding how some victims failed to see the warning signs can be extremely difficult, particularly for someone who has not been through any remotely similar experience. However, we should avoid being too judgmental. Many things that were not at all apparent at the time can be seen in hindsight:

Barbara was loyal to Brent for more than five years and says she would have given her life for him, although in all those years they seldom spent a holiday or birthday together and she seldom received a birthday or Christmas present from him.

He would conveniently disappear on such occasions, telling her that they "stressed him out" so he couldn't "handle them." She believed him because she wanted to believe him, but now acknowledges that his behavior indicated his lack of commitment to their relationship; it indicated his selfishness and the existence of a hidden agenda.

Thelma dated Bill exclusively for five years, even though he never allowed her to leave any of her belongings at his home. When she did, he got extremely upset and even threw some of her things away.

However, Thelma accepted Bill's explanation that this attitude was just his personal quirk. Only later did she realize that it was more likely he had different women visiting his apartment and didn't want them finding evidence of each other.

Steve was emotionally raped by Ellen, who had been married twice before and told him she had used her first marriage only to escape from a particularly difficult situation. She also told him she had an affair during her second marriage with one of her early acting instructors, a married man with several children.

However, Ellen excused her past actions by telling Steve that her second husband had been an active bisexual and an alcoholic who was frequently drunk and often very depressed. Steve wanted to believe her and did so.

Cheryl was driven almost to suicide by Robert's callous exploitation. Yet she had been warned about his true nature by his aunt, who advised her in no uncertain terms not to marry him

His aunt told Cheryl he would ruin her and take her home and business. Cheryl recalls how she simply would not believe what she was hearing: "I thought Robert would be different for me. I loved him and didn't see him the way he really was."

Fortunately, she didn't marry him. If she had, her recovery would have been complicated by legal and financial stress, in addition to the emotional trauma.

Watch for Telltale Signs

Emotional rapists generally don't give many clues about what they are really like, but they may show signs of their true selves, although these signs are not like red flashing lights and it's often only after the rape is revealed that their real significance becomes apparent.

We can detect these telltale signals if we look out for them and are willing to recognize them for what they really are, not what we want them to be. A little open-minded observation can go a long way:

- If someone has a history of sexual affairs, don't assume he or she will change just for your relationship, or be any more loyal to you.
- Listen to what your partner tells you about previous relationships, what happened and why.
- See how he or she treats and relates to others, because that's how he or she will treat you at some time in the future.

What are this person's values? Is he or she:

- honest—or a bit too creative with the truth?
- thoughtful and considerate—or inclined to self-centered behavior?
- loyal and monogamous—or rather too ready to flirt at every opportunity?
- kind and generous—or occasionally cruel and mean?
- direct—or manipulative?

How does he or she treat others? Children, parents, employees or co-workers? Does he or she:

- use physical appeal to get what he or she wants?
- admit when he or she is wrong, or blame others?
- keep agreements?
- show up on time and call if he or she will be late?
- do what he or she agreed to do?
- avoid clarity in agreements?
- reciprocate—or are you always picking up the tab?

Proceed With Caution

If you are already involved with someone, remember that an emotional rapist is usually skilled at changing the basis of a relationship.

It is important to be aware of the broad pattern of your life, not just the day-to-day details.

- Keep an eye on the "trends," not just where you and your partner happen to be at any one moment.
- Consider keeping a personal diary, noting any subtle but significant changes in your relationship. Are things being kept on a value-for-value basis or are you gradually giving more and receiving less?
- Take some time regularly to review your observations, and be willing to believe that, if things are changing for the worse in some areas, the chances are that trend is not suddenly going to be reversed.

If you are newly involved with someone but are contemplating a more serious commitment, consider:

- Does that person have any obvious vested interests in the relationship?
- Does he or she stand to gain more than love by entering into a relationship with you? If so, you may need to discuss value-for-value commitments, and put some agreements in writing.

    This may make you feel uncomfortable but it is far less painful than emotional rape, and if your partner is honest and sincere, without any hidden agenda, reaching a clear understanding about the basis of your relationship will invariably be welcomed.

Whatever the status of your relationship:

- Listen to others. If your friends and family are telling you to be careful, hear them out. Sometimes people who are not involved in a situation are able to see what you can't. If they don't volunteer an opinion, be sure to ask for it.

Finally, be cautious if someone seems too good to be true.

It is one of the "skills" of emotional rapists to make themselves appear to be whatever their victim wants them to be. Few people are perfect, so proceed with caution if you meet anyone who appears to embody everything you ever wanted in a partner.

This doesn't mean don't proceed. It means be cautious. Most people are not emotional rapists and there is no need to become paranoid about the motives of everyone you meet. The value of self-defense is that it enables us to enjoy a life that includes love and trust, not a life based on fear.

Love is Blind

Whoever coined the phrase "Love is Blind" had a shrewd understanding of human relations. It's a maxim that has stood the test of time, and for good reason.

We know we are powerless to resist the HALF factors (Health, Achievement, Love, and Faith) and, although most people are honest and sincere, there are some who will take advantage of our powerlessness.

This can happen in our homes, at work, even at our places of worship. Consider the mass suicide of the followers of Jim Jones at Jonestown in the 1970s, a tragic illustration of the extent of powerlessness.

Interestingly, most people now see the Jonestown incident as an isolated event, precipitated by circumstances that would never be able to influence their behavior. They tell themselves they would never give anyone that much power over them. But it is a dangerous mistake to underestimate powerlessness.

Thousands of young people were sent to kill and be killed in Vietnam, persuaded to answer their country's call by appeals to their senses of patriotism, honor, bravery, and duty; all forms of love and achievement. Most did it without question. Surely there are clear parallels here with the events at Jonestown.

Draw Up a HALF Checklist

From time to time, draw up a HALF checklist, and have the courage to be honest with yourself.

Examine each HALF factor (Health, Achievement, Love, and Faith) separately and dispassionately, and ask questions. Is your relationship balanced? Is value-for-value being maintained?

Take out a piece of blank paper and draw a line down the middle. On one side, list everything you are getting out of your relationship; on the other side, write down how your partner is benefiting.

Make sure you distinguish between promises and what is actually happening right now. If your lover or spouse is getting an education or starting a business at your expense, on the understanding that you will somehow benefit financially in the future, that's only a promise—one that may or may not be fulfilled.

A legal form of ownership, like stock, or some written agreement, is preferable to a verbal promise. There's no guarantee that just before he or she passes final exams with top marks, or the business takes off in a big way, you won't be told there's been a, unilaterally declared, change of plans: "Things are different now...I'm bored...good-bye."

Love neither can nor should be evaluated on a profit-and-loss balance sheet. There is nothing inherently wrong with giving more than you receive. Indeed, it can be beautiful and enriching, as long as you know that is what you are doing and recognize there are never any guarantees that a relationship will work out as planned.

The process of checking value-for-value ensures

only that you are fully aware of the basis of your relationship, that you are not being taken advantage of, and are not taking advantage of someone else.

Head Off Dangerous Situations

One simple precaution to reduce the risk of being assaulted, sexually or otherwise, is to avoid placing yourself in vulnerable situations.

Commonsense dictates that you don't go walking alone through the worst, badly lit sections of town in the early hours of the morning. That's a very high-risk situation. The same commonsense rule—not to expose yourself to unnecessary risks—applies to relationships.

One way to avoid emotional rape in marriage is to marry someone of approximately equal means. If both you and your spouse have similar assets and income there is less chance of there being any hidden agenda concerned with financial gain.

Nowadays it is quite common, and eminently sensible, to ask your intended for a detailed financial statement and have it checked out by an accountant. (You should, of course, provide the same information about your own financial situation.)

It may be a chilling commentary on current attitudes to marriage and honesty in relations with others, but such apparently cold considerations need not compromise or jeopardize your romantic relationship. Indeed, more often than not they are welcomed by both parties, assuming neither has anything to hide.

The State and Your Union

If your financial situations are not equal, discuss value-for-value and consider making a prenuptial agreement.

Be sure to employ an attorney and that you understand the legal ramifications of marriage, community property, and all public policies recognized in the state where the ceremony will take place. In some states you cannot completely protect yourself by drawing up a prenuptial agreement and it is wise to consult an attorney about specific state laws governing marriage and divorce before saying "I do."

Certain states have public policies against waiving spousal support, for example, a situation that could prove critical if your income is significantly greater than that of your intended. Spousal support is based more on income than assets.

It is also vitally important that your intended obtains his or her own independent legal counsel before signing any prenuptial agreement, otherwise the terms of the agreement can be successfully challenged on the basis that he or she was "uninformed."

Pay Attention—and Take Your Time

If you have been in a relationship for more than a year and it seems unbalanced and getting worse, you have a responsibility to yourself to confront the situation.

■ Even if you do not see yourself likely to suffer any tangible losses by continuing in the relationship, ask yourself whether you are willing to lose more of that most precious commodity: time.

Only you can decide whether you can afford to lose years of your personal or professional life.

■ Further, ask yourself whether you can cope with the trauma of emotional rape and what it will cost you.

The longer a potentially disastrous situation continues, the more severe will be the physical and emotional consequences.

■ There is sure to be pain, but when you recognize the

signs that your partner is an emotional rapist, and you have protected yourself as best you can, be ready and willing to drive him or her out of your life.

This means being willing to accept the pain of ending what was, to you, the most intimate and important relationship in your life—while the situation is still manageable and survivable.

Pay attention to your inner voices. Survivors of emotional and sexual rape frequently admit after the event that they heard inner voices warning them of potential disaster, but that their rational mind had talked them out of heeding their subconscious concerns.

One survivor, Maureen, recalled several instances when she had instinctively felt the desire to get out of her marriage for her own safety. In those brief moments she couldn't bring herself to wear her wedding ring. However, she let her feelings show and her emotional rapist, chameleon-like, quickly camouflaged his true self. With no tangible evidence, Maureen did nothing to protect herself, a failure that resulted in a much more costly experience, both financially and emotionally, years later.

If something is bothering you, at gut level, it never hurts to check it out.

Move slowly into new relationships:

■ Date non-exclusively for a certain time before making a commitment to date exclusively. Then...

■ ...date exclusively for a good period of time before living together. Then...

■ ...live together for a few years before getting married.

Living with someone before getting married is an excellent protective measure, although it doesn't guarantee that the marriage will be successful. It gives partners a chance to learn more about each other's values, commitment to career (if any), to friends and family...and, most importantly, to each other.

Pre-Marital Safety

Living together also gives two people an opportunity to determine each other's financial situation and attitude toward money; so if you do make plans to get married you'll both know exactly what issues to address in any prenuptial agreement.

If your intended is not your financial equal and resists the idea of a prenuptial agreement, you might want to ask him or her why, and ask yourself whether you should go ahead with your marriage plans.

- Before marriage, it is a good idea to keep money, property and credit cards separate.

- On the day before you get married, make sure you can document exactly what you have, and consider whether you want to co-mingle your assets after marriage.

- If you have a large amount of cash in the bank consider investing it in a good mutual fund, in your name only, before your wedding day. Keep it separate from community funds and assets. Once you co-mingle your cash or assets, in most states they become community property.

Examine your reasons for entering into the legal relationship of marriage.

The fact that you love each other is not necessarily sufficient in itself; getting married does not guarantee improving the quality of your love or commitment to each other.

Marriage as a legal relationship has nothing to do with love, it has to do with law. So the question is, What is it you want to do that requires the legal relationship of marriage? You may want to have children, for example, which might be considered a valid reason for marriage—but it's not a legal requirement.

On top of the terrible emotional trauma involved in separation and divorce, financial losses can be absolutely crushing, causing often irreparable damage,

generally to the partner who has most to lose in terms of cash and material assets.

It makes sense to protect yourself against such a possibility, which is why any discussion of self-defense is inevitably going to be preoccupied, perhaps to an almost unseemly extent, with safety measures to protect financial interests.

Put it in Writing

Emotional rapists hate clarity, preferring as much room as possible to maneuver.

When an agreement is legally recorded in writing the onus is on the rapist to prove it is not valid.

This doesn't mean that because someone has put something in writing they are not an emotional rapist. Anyone can challenge anything in court, and even if the action is unsuccessful the financial and emotional cost of mounting your defense can be considerable. In the celebrated separation of multi-millionaire financier Donald Trump from his wife Ivana, Mrs. Trump demonstrated that even the legality of prenuptial and post nuptial agreements signed after advice from teams of expensive attorneys can be challenged.

Employ an attorney to make sure that, as far as is possible, any such agreement is legally watertight. And, again, make sure both parties to the agreement have independent legal counsel.

Oral agreements have no legal value. Any agreement of any significance should be set out in writing, witnessed, or recorded on tape. Check with an attorney about specific state laws, particularly laws governing tape-recorded verbal agreements. In most states recordings of telephone conversations are not admissible as evidence unless the other party was informed the conversation was being recorded.

Think Ahead and Stay Cool

The best time to plan for any emergency is before it happens—because if it does, you may not be able to think or act very clearly. Even if you are happy and secure in your current relationship, it's worth running through your own emergency survival plan.

If your loving relationship broke up tomorrow:
- How would you stand up emotionally?
- Who would you turn to for emotional support?
- Would you be out on a financial limb?
- Would you cope, or go into a state of depression or rage?

In Chapter Three we saw how Barbara improved her chances for recovery by keeping cool. She instinctively knew something was wrong in her relationship with Brent but didn't confront him until she had hard evidence; obtained in her case by a private detective she hired to follow Brent on his mysterious absences from home.

Even when armed with the facts, Barbara didn't engineer a major confrontation. She simply asked Brent whether he was involved with another woman. When he not only lied, but also reassured her that he still loved her, she learned a lot more about herself and their relationship than she would if she had confronted him.

She learned that Brent was such an accomplished deceiver that she couldn't tell whether he was telling the truth or lying, and because she didn't tell Brent what she knew, or how she knew it, she continued to gather information that proved invaluable to her recovery.

Take Action on Your Own Terms

If you're in a legal relationship, such as marriage, with an emotional rapist don't begin legal action as soon as you realize what is happening. Don't mention divorce

or separation, and don't physically separate unless it
is absolutely necessary. Instead, make a calm assess-
ment of your situation.

Consider the financial and emotional implications.
Consult an attorney, a financial adviser, a psychologist,
perhaps a private detective, to arm yourself with as many
facts as possible before hostilities are openly declared.

Typically, emotional rapists are passive/active and will
try to manipulate their victims into precipitating what they
want to happen, such as the end of the relationship. Don't
play into their hands.

It may be very difficult to bide your time, particularly
when you realize that you have been used, but it can be
more painful, legally and emotionally, to react without
planning. By overreacting you would probably be helping
the rapist again to fulfill his or her hidden agenda by your
appearing to cause the breakup of the relationship.

Selection and Screening

"You can't cheat an honest man" is an old adage, but unfortunately it isn't always true. Bad things do happen to
good people, and honest people do get cheated; in fact,
they are usually the most trusting and this makes them
easier targets for exploitation.

However, if our personal value system is solid it offers
useful protection:

- If Steve (Chapter One) had placed loyalty and faithful-
  ness higher on his list of values, he might never have
  become involved with Ellen, a woman whom he knew
  had extramarital affairs and had abandoned her previous husband, despite the fact he was ill.

- If Cheryl (Chapter Two) had placed less importance on
  physical attractiveness and more on the values of honesty and integrity, it's unlikely that she would have been
  deceived by Robert. By her own admission he was clearly

a superficial, materialistic character and, although she might still have been physically attracted to him, she probably wouldn't have become so emotionally involved.

When we are considering our relationships, on any level, with other people, values have to become part of our selection and screening process. This applies to our relations with friends, family, co-workers, everyone we meet, and is most important when we are contemplating lasting involvement with another person in an intimate one-on-one relationship like marriage.

Superficial considerations, such as looks, don't have to be ignored; in fact, we probably couldn't exclude them altogether from our appreciation of others. But we must include other factors.

Having a clear system of values enables us to begin to see other people for their true selves:

- It helps us to recognize the small signals in a person's everyday behavior and attitudes as significant indications of that person's true nature.

- It helps us to see behind the superficial mask to know the person within—and, if necessary, to avoid further involvement before that person can cause irreparable damage to our life.

Blueprint for a Rape-Free Society 15

What's in a Name?

There's a theory that when you know the true name for something, you take away any power it has over you. If only it were that simple. We know the names of many things that continue to haunt and torment us: greed, poverty, child abuse, racial prejudice, war... the list, unfortunately, seems endless.

Nevertheless, identifying something—giving a particular area of human experience a name—does enable us to address the problem, to begin examining and discussing it. It's an essential, positive first step toward solving it.

Naming is perhaps the most important part of our blueprint for a rape-free society. The main purpose of this book is to identify emotional rape: to bring it into the open, examine what causes it, and learn how to take away any power it has over us.

In earlier chapters we looked at emotional rape and the individual. Then we discussed how the macro forces at work in society—specifically, in the mass media, the medical profession and the education and legal systems—sanction and promote emotional rape.

What follows is a, far from exhaustive, list of suggestions as to how we might act to eliminate this trauma from our society...

The Media Message

Recall the Phil Donahue program discussed in Chapter Eleven. The topic was "How To Marry Rich," and the special guest was a woman who held workshops on finding a wealthy mate; an idea apparently endorsed by Donahue, who skillfully repelled all critical comments from his audience.

Within a year the same woman appeared on the Sally Jessy Raphael talk show and, after an introductory discussion, Sally prepared to take audience questions. However, she prefaced this open-forum part of her show by remarking that many people would surely take issue with her guest's marry-for-money philosophy. And she also introduced a second female guest, the editor of *Self* magazine, who expressed the opinion that marrying for money was a repugnant idea.

The difference in the treatment of the same theme on the two shows was striking, illustrating how the chosen angle of approach can radically affect the message communicated to the viewing public.

One show seemed to sanction the notion of marrying for money, the use of another person's higher emotions for personal gain. The other treated the notion with the seriousness it deserves, and abhorred and rejected such behavior.

The Responsible Approach

The mass media sends out powerful messages, many of them involving the affirmation of amoral codes of behavior.

Creative artists would argue in their own defense, of course, that they are simply reflecting society as it is, which is a fair point. But it is one that does not, in itself, justify their endeavors. As well as *reflecting* society, those decision-makers in the media also have a duty to acknowledge their role as powerful opinion-*formers*. Theirs is a heavy responsibility indeed. Fundamentally, the issue is how certain subjects, situations and values are treated; the all-important angle of approach.

The moguls of Hollywood and the television industry dictate the nature of the most influential mass media messages that are rife in our society.

They have the power to make a positive difference in the way we think and behave. Therefore they have a responsibility to produce popular entertainment that not only makes money but also directs society's value system towards good rather than evil.

Writers of popular songs, stories and books, editors and publishers of magazines, radio broadcasters and producers all share that responsibility.

Accepting Our Powerlessness

The "Just Say No" campaign completely failed to grasp the fundamental characteristic of the nation's drug problem—powerlessness—by suggesting addicts have a choice; that they're able to choose, "Yes" or "No."

As long as we propagate the notion that we are all in control, that we have a choice about everything in our lives, the more time it will take to significantly reduce the drug problem in this country—and to make people aware of the nature of emotional rape.

The reality that we are powerless to resist the HALF factors (Health, Achievement, Love, and Faith) has to be open to discussion, not implicitly denied.

We must recognize that it's not a matter of "Just Saying No." A more appropriate slogan might be, "Just Say Help."

Society should ensure, of course, that help is widely available for those who need it, whether they are battling addiction, to drugs or alcohol, for example, or trying to cope with the trauma of emotional rape.

The Marital Commitment

The marriage contract also needs to reflect what it is: a legal contract, with broad implications for the future of your personal life and finances.

In any other area of life where such a momentous commitment is being contemplated, the purchase of a new home or signing of a big business deal, for instance, lengthy documents set forth all the terms and conditions. The small print is thoroughly scrutinized by all parties concerned, or more probably by their attorneys, before anyone considers putting pen to paper.

Why should our approach to marriage be different?

Simply to set forth all the legal implications of getting married would not compromise the feelings of love and respect each party presumably has for the other. Indeed, going ahead with the marriage, with each partner having full knowledge of the implications of that course, would bear testimony to the strength of those feelings.

Marriage should not be for the fainthearted, nor should it be for the reckless or uninformed.

The emphasis of the marriage contract should be on making each partner fully aware; on ensuring that

we only enter into marriage when we fully appreciate its seriousness.

Such an appreciation would provide a sound foundation for a couple's future happiness and avoid much unhappiness by deterring those who had not thought enough about the extent of the marriage commitment.

Recognizing Legal Reality

When considering any reform of the ceremony and contract of marriage, a useful "mission statement" might be: To make marriage as much hassle to get into as it is to get out of.

Prenuptial agreements need to become legally required rather than remaining an option taken up by a minority.

Both partners need to be made aware of the laws relating to marriage, to understand what they are really agreeing to: What exactly is spousal support? Community property? Community income? No-fault divorce? Public policy?

The marriage license should not be a license to commit emotional rape any more than it is a license to commit sexual rape.

One Person Can Make a Difference: The Bumblebee Effect

The scientific discipline known as the Chaos Theory emphasizes the influence on our lives of the "Bumblebee Effect." Devotees proclaim that apparently random, unrelated actions have an effect throughout the rest of the world. A bumblebee flapping its wings in Europe, the argument runs, might result in a tornado in the United States.

Without debating the finer points of this notion, the

significant part of the thesis is that, although it may appear that our efforts as individuals have no useful effect, they really do. The individual has considerable power to change things just by "spreading the word"; by explaining to others that emotional rape is wrong, and asking them to give their friends and family the same message.

Consider a mathematical model: On day one, a single individual tells two other people a particular thing. On day two those two people go out and each tells two others that thing. On day three those four people each tell two others...and so on. Incredible as it may seem, everyone on this planet would receive this message in just thirty-three days.

If the message is important enough, it can be communicated quickly, becoming a powerful force for social change.

The individual can make a difference. How we all live—the values we live by and the way we behave— can have a tremendous influence on social mores. In this we *do* bear a responsibility for what happens in society; and, therefore, what happens to us.

Take Courage

Impressive though this mathematical example undoubtedly is, it cannot, of course, be directly applied to real life. Human communication doesn't work in strict unbroken sequences, nor does it conform to the principles of multiplication theory.

Nevertheless the model is well worth remembering in our daily lives; in our irregular, haphazard, random interaction with others:

We need to feel responsible for evil on an individual level, aware that we have to oppose it wherever and whenever it is encountered.

Day by day we can combat evil with personal courage and goodness:

- We can constantly remind ourselves and each other about right and wrong, about what kind of behavior is acceptable and what is not;
- We can be ready and willing to offer support to survivors of evil;
- We can challenge those whom we see behaving unacceptably, and not be content to stand idly by for fear of getting involved;
- We can let it be known that we cannot tolerate people using other people's higher emotions for personal gain;
- We can be careful not to mislead others, or to allow them to misunderstand our feelings towards them.

We need to be aware that evil exists like a contagious virus, and has a very real effect on the health of individuals and of society as a whole. We can either stop it, or we can transmit it.

If we accept personal responsibility for evil, it can be effectively countered and contained. If our attitude is irresponsible—if we ignore its existence, or believe that it doesn't concern us—evil will surely continue to spread.

Inspiring Moments—Abiding Memories

In 1989 the fears which most Californians live with every day became a reality. A severe earthquake hit the San Francisco area. It was rush hour, all power supplies were cut off, all the traffic signals stopped functioning. It was a potentially chaotic situation.

However, many observers (myself included) later recalled how people got out of their cars and took it upon themselves to direct the traffic at busy intersections, trying to restore some semblance of order. Far from becoming agitated and abusive towards other drivers, motorists waited patiently in their vehicles on the clogged freeways and streets, responding courteously to the efforts of those who were trying to get things moving again.

In some of the areas hit by the earthquake, power supplies were out for days, yet there were few reports of looting or other public disorder. In fact, many of those who were arrested during that time were people who had tried to cross police lines to help rescue others they knew were still trapped in the rubble.

Very few people chose to take advantage of the situation, preferring instead to help each other without being asked—almost instinctively. Amid all the turmoil and disruption it was an inspiring, positive illustration of what is possible.

The same year there was a second such illustration during the student-led pro-democracy demonstrations in Tiananmen Square in Beijing, China. It was a moment captured by photographers and became a symbol of the courageous opposition to a harsh and repressive regime.

One solitary protester stood defiantly in front of a column of government tanks, challenging them either to halt their advance, or to run him over.

The tanks halted in the middle of the road, just a few feet from this solitary human roadblock who had the courage to challenge those soldiers to recognize that what they were doing was wrong.

It takes similar courage to stand in the way of emotional rape. On the face of it there is little to be gained and probably a lot to lose; all we may achieve is to alienate ourselves from others, perhaps our friends, if we confront them about what they are doing.

Nevertheless, almost every one of us knows someone who is playing this game, who is using somebody else to some degree, and we should not wait until the situation becomes desperate before making our stand.

This one unidentified protester in Tiananmen Square

was not alone in his bravery and determination to stand up for basic human values.

Unseen by the cameras, the officer commanding the leading tank also displayed immense courage. He decided that, whatever reprisals the military hierarchy or political bureaucrats might take, he could not be responsible for the cold-blooded murder of another individual. The brakes were applied.

During that period of protests, troops from the same geographical areas as the demonstrators also refused to open fire upon their countrymen. (The peaceful protests were eventually brought to a violent end by soldiers transported from bases in distant cantons, who had no natural empathy with the demonstrators.)

In these instances, the essential goodness of the individual came to the fore when it really counted—in adversity. It can serve us well, too, in opposing the spread of evil in society, whether that evil manifests itself as emotional rape or any other major threat to the social good.

We have to find the courage to get involved and to stand up to those who would use the best and highest human qualities, such as the ability to love and trust, for their own narcissistic gain.

Bibliography

Carnegie, Dale. *How To Win Friends and Influence People.* New York, NY: Simon & Schuster, 1936-1981.

Dyer, Dr. Wayne. *You'll See It When You Believe It.* New York, NY: William Morrow and Company Inc., 1989.

Eliot, Dr. Robert S., and Dennis L. Breo. *Is It Worth Dying For?* New York, NY: Bantam Books, 1989.

Fox, Emmet. *The Ten Commandments.* San Francisco, CA: Harper & Row, 1953.

Frankl, Victor. *Man's Search for Meaning.* Boston, Mass.: Beacon Press, 1959.

Fromm, Erich. *The Art of Loving.* New York, NY: Harper & Row, 1956.

Gatto, John. *Dumbing Us Down.* Available direct from the author: 235 W. 76th Street, New York, NY, 10023.

Hoyle, Sir Fred., and N. C. Wickramasinghe. *Evolution From Space.* New York, NY: Simon & Schuster, 1981.

Kingma, Daphne Rose. *Coming Apart—Why Relationships End and How To Live Through the Ending of Yours.* Berkeley, CA: Conari Press, 1987.

Kubler-Ross, Elisabeth. *Death—The Final Stage of Growth.* New York, NY: Simon & Schuster, 1976.

Kushner, Harold S. *When Bad Things Happen to Good People.* New York, NY: Avon Books, 1981. By the same author: *When All You've Ever Wanted Isn't Enough,* New York, NY: Simon & Schuster, 1986; and *Who Needs God?,* New York, NY: Simon & Schuster, 1991.

Liberman, Dr. Jacob. *Light—Medicine of the Future.* Santa Fe, NM: Bear and Company, 1991.

Ludwig, Dr. Arnold. *Understanding The Alcoholic's Mind.* New York, NY: Oxford Press, 1988.

Maslow, Abraham. *Toward a Psychology of Being.* New York, NY: D. Van Nostrand Company, 1968.

Moody Jr., Dr. Raymond A. *The Light Beyond.* New York, NY: Bantam Books, 1988.

O'Brien, D. *Two of a Kind—The Hillside Stranglers.* New York, NY: Signet, 1989.

Reiff, Robert. *The Invisible Victim.* New York, NY: Basic Books Inc., 1979.

Ringer, Robert J. *Looking Out For #1.* New York, NY: Fawcett Crest, 1977. By the same author: *Living Without Limits*, Nightingale Conant, 1988, (800) 323-5552.

Rubin, Dr. Theodore Isaac. *Real Love.* New York, NY: Continuum, 1990.

Scott Peck, Dr. M. *The People of the Lie.* New York, NY: Simon & Schuster, 1983.

Szasz, Thomas. *Heresies.* New York, NY: Anchor Books, 1976.

Walsh, Dr. Anthony. *Human Nature and Love.* Washington DC: University Press of America, 1981.

Warshaw, Robin. *I Never Called It Rape.* New York, NY: Harper and Row, 1988.

Wilson Schaef, Anne. *When Society Becomes an Addict.* San Francisco, CA: Harper and Row, 1987. By the same author, with Fassel, Diane: *The Addictive Organization.* Harper & Row, San Francisco, CA: 1988.